THE AUTO ALBUM

Also by Tad Burness

American Car Spotter's Guide, 1920–1939

American Car Spotter's Guide, 1940–1965

American Car Spotter's Guide, 1966–1980

Chevy Spotter's Guide, 1920–1980

Ford Spotter's Guide, 1920–1980

Imported Car Spotter's Guide

American Truck Spotter's Guide, 1920–1970

American Pick-up and Van Spotter's Guide, 1945–1982

Cars of the Early Twenties

Cars of the Early Thirties

Indianapolis 500 Winners

Tad Burness

THE AUTO ALBUM

HOUGHTON MIFFLIN COMPANY BOSTON 1983

Library of Congress Cataloging in Publication Data

Burness, Tad, date
The Auto album.
Collection of automobile drawings from the author's
nationally syndicated newspaper feature.
1. Automobiles — History. 2. Automobiles — Drawings.
I. Title.
TL15.B9   1983   629.2′222′0973   82-23227
ISBN 0-395-33966-9 (pbk.)

Printed in the United States of America

1 2 3 4 5 6 7 8 9 10 V

I lovingly dedicate this book to my wife, Sandy; to my daughter, Tammy; to my mother, Wallea B. Draper; and to all the friends and relatives who encouraged me on this project.

CONTENTS

Limitations and a Growing Environmental Awareness (The 1960s and 1970s)

INTRODUCTION

"Auto Album" pictures and stories have appeared in many newspapers each week since 1966, presenting a different vehicle each time. There have been numerous requests for a new book of prints from the series, so I've selected some highlights from the column's past twelve years.

Along with the stories that accompany each car or truck, there are also introductory notes for each decade or era, to help give a feeling of what was going on in the world during those years.

I hope that the book will evoke pleasant memories for you or teach you some interesting facts about these unusual vehicles and their times.

Should you have any questions or comments about this book or about old cars in general, you're invited to write to me, Tad Burness, c/o *The Auto Album*, Houghton Mifflin Company, 2 Park Street, Boston, Massachusetts 02108.

I'll be happy to reply if you'll kindly enclose a self-addressed, stamped envelope with your letter.

Tad Burness
Pacific Grove, California

THE AUTO ALBUM

Though a few experimental "horseless carriages" were built before 1890, it was the final decade of the old century that became the "pioneer" era for self-propelled automobiles, that saw the first commercial sales of autos to private individuals.

Needless to say, the first automobiles were expensive, being produced in very limited numbers, and were considered nothing more than playthings for the wealthy. Some were imported to the United States from France, where auto production had a head start. The early cars were, in some cases, motorized buggies. Though some were gas-driven, others used steam or electricity as a power source, such as the 1894 Electrobat and the 1903 White Steamer.

Because many people depended on the railroads for transportation between towns, and on electric streetcars for citywide travel, the new automobiles did not seem necessary at first. They frightened horses along country lanes, and some towns required any horseless carriage to be preceded by a man on foot, carrying a red warning flag or lantern!

Oldsmobile is the most established of today's remaining brands, having opened shop in 1897. The Ford Motor Company was established officially in 1903, and in October 1908, Henry Ford launched his historical Model T series, the line of cars most responsible for popularizing the family car.

Before 1910, much wood was used to build auto bodies; not only the framework was wooden but often the exterior panels were as well. Engines usually had one to four cylinders and were noisy and undependable.

The U.S. Presidents during this era of the automobile industry's infancy were: Benjamin Harrison (1889–1893), Grover Cleveland (1893–1897; his second term), William McKinley (1897–1901), Theodore Roosevelt (1901–1909), and William H. Taft (1909–1913).

The most notable President was "TR," Teddy Roosevelt, who as Vice-President succeeded McKinley upon his assassination. TR's foreign policy motto was "Speak softly, but carry a big stick," and during his administration the United States became the most dominant power in the Western Hemisphere and grew in influence overseas.

The 1890s — the last decade of the Victorian era — was known for its mannered and genteel way of life among the middle and upper social classes, for its heavy, frilly women's fashions, and for elaborate, decorative architecture and home furnishings. The tall and stately Victorian homes were built of wood, with many rooms, nooks, and crannies and much decorative trim (known in the building trade as gingerbread). Indoor plumbing was available, though in rural areas it was often considered an unnecessary luxury. When there was no plumbing, a little outhouse graced the back yard.

Though Thomas Edison had invented the phonograph in 1877, cylinder records were not available to the public until the late 1890s, and flat disc records came with the twentieth century. Until then, popular music was promoted in stage comedies and by traveling vaudeville and minstrel shows and circulated by sheet music to be played on home pianos.

Among the song hits of the 1890s and 1900s were: "A Bicycle Built for Two" (1892), "The Sidewalks of New York" (1894), "The Stars and Stripes Forever" (1897), "My Wild Irish Rose" (1899), "A Bird in a Gilded Cage" (1900), "In the Good Old Summertime" (1902), "Meet Me in St. Louis" (1904), "In My Merry Oldsmobile" (1905), "My Gal Sal" (1905), "Red Wing" (1907), "Shine On, Harvest Moon" (1908), and "Put On Your Old Grey Bonnet" (1909).

The Antique Era

To 1909

1894 Electrobat

The Electrobat is one of the rarest, least-known antique cars; few auto historians have ever heard of it.

The horse and buggy still dominated short-distance American transportation in 1894, the year of the first Electrobat. This horseless carriage, with its hard-riding spoke wheels, used a doorbell for a horn, as did other pioneer electric cars.

The builders were trained men: Henry G. Morris was a mechanical engineer and Pedro G. Salom was an electrician.

Their second vehicle was entered in the *Chicago Tribune Herald* 1895 Automobile Race. It did not finish, but it was awarded a gold medal for quietness of operation and for design. The winner of the race, and of its $2000 prize, was a Duryea car.

The second Electrobat managed to exceed its top speed of 25 miles an hour in September 1896 at another race in Providence, Rhode Island.

The Electrobat was an almost forgotten car, but a clear photograph and written details were published in 1949 in the commemorative program of the Philadelphia Auto Show.

The Electrobat was also known as the Morris & Salom car. Additional cars were reportedly produced until 1897.

The car illustrated here had two electric motors, whereas most electric cars used only one!

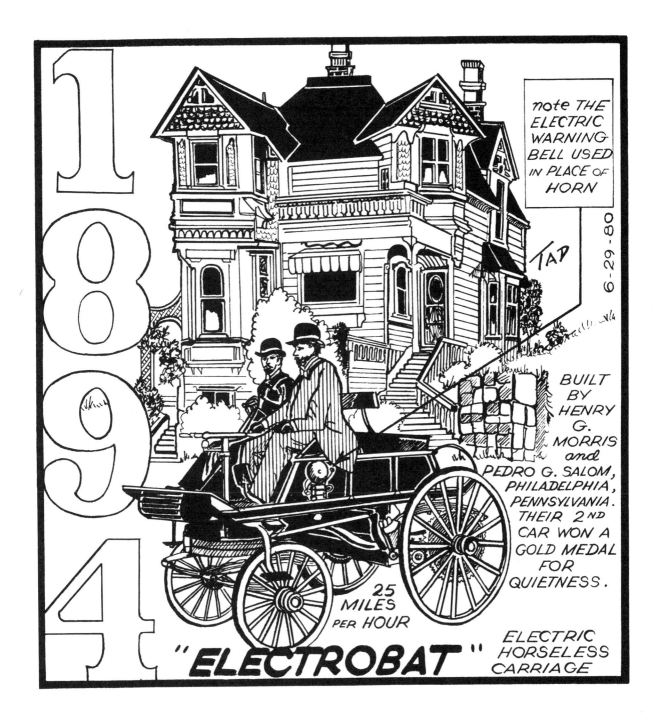

1903 White Steam Car

This White Steamer, for 1903, carried many new features.

The 1902 White Model B Stanhope had been a buggy-style, curved-dash, 7-horsepower runabout with wire wheels and a simple tiller for steering control: a typical, old-fashioned "horseless carriage."

But the Model C for 1903 offered an improved compound engine in front, under the new hood; a steering wheel; a driveshaft; an optional canopy top; and many extras. A big change from the "B," it rode on wood artillery wheels.

However, there had been an experimental, transitional White Elephant special of 1902, which did have a hood in front as well as other features that were to go into regular production for 1903.

The original company began in 1859, when Thomas H. White, of Templeton, Massachusetts, first manufactured sewing machines. In 1863 he moved his operations to Orange, and in 1866 he moved to Cleveland, Ohio, which became the home of the White Sewing Machine Company (reorganized under this name in 1876, the year of America's Centennial).

An experimental steam car was built in 1899, and at the turn of the century motor cars and trucks joined sewing machines as products manufactured by White.

The White Motor Corporation is also known for its fine trucks, buses, and other commercial vehicles. In recent years, White's varied line of trucks have included the White Freightliner and Western Star series.

1907 Thomas Flyer

This Thomas Flyer won the famous New York–Paris race in 1908.

Six cars competed. In addition to the Thomas (built in the U.S.), there was the German Protos, the Italian Brixia-Zust, and three French cars: the De Dion–Bouton, the Motobloc, and the smallest car in the race, the Sizaire-Naudin.

The body and fenders of the Thomas Flyer were altered for the race. In fact, all the cars looked as homely as peddlers' wagons, laden down with items needed for the long trip.

The first car to get in trouble was the Brixia-Zust, which broke a transmission chain and suffered a cracked radiator not long after the race began. But it was repaired.

A blizzard hampered the cars only twenty miles from the starting point.

And because of the poor roads in 1908, there were many pitfalls along the way.

Going west across the United States, the Thomas got ahead. Meanwhile, the Sizaire-Naudin had quit the race after less than 100 miles because a gear broke in the rear axle and no spare parts were available. In Cedar Rapids, Iowa, the Motobloc was withdrawn because its team became discouraged.

From San Francisco, the Thomas was carried by boat to Alaska. But after it reached port on April 8, the officials decided that melting snows would make an Alaskan crossing impossible.

Forewarned, the Brixia-Zust and De Dion teams were allowed to bypass the planned Alaska route and were instead shipped from Seattle to Japan. The Protos was shipped to Russia, after a temporary disqualification, bypassing Japan.

Though the Protos was the first car to reach Paris, on July 26, the Thomas won by decision because it was the only car that had attempted the full original route.

1908 Rapid Bus (Sightseeing Car)

This Rapid Bus, originally known as a "Sightseeing Car," was quite an outlandish, peculiar-looking vehicle, with an awkward, cratelike design.

In 1900, according to historians, Morris and Max Grabowsky began building their first motor truck in Detroit; in 1902, a sale was made and more trucks were built, as the Grabowsky enterprise was reorganized as the Rapid Motor Vehicle Company. However, there was still a Grabowsky Power Wagon Company in business in Detroit as late as the early teen years. Sightseeing buses were built under the Grabowsky name as well.

"Built for Business," the Rapid Sightseeing Car was advertised as a real money-making proposition, since the buyer of one of these vehicles could use it to earn from "$100 to $500 a week" or "$12 an hour" — a virtual fortune in 1908, when many clerks and factory workers were happy to receive 25 cents an hour.

As the ads promised, "There is an opportunity everywhere — scarcely a city, town or village in the United States where a Rapid Pullman Sightseeing Car cannot be run at a great profit." In those times, bus franchises and business license requirements were unnecessary in many places.

In 1908, a Rapid ad read "12 passengers, $1 apiece, $12 — eight loads a day, $96 cash — 6 days in the week, $576." Thus, many little bus and jitney companies sprang into existence.

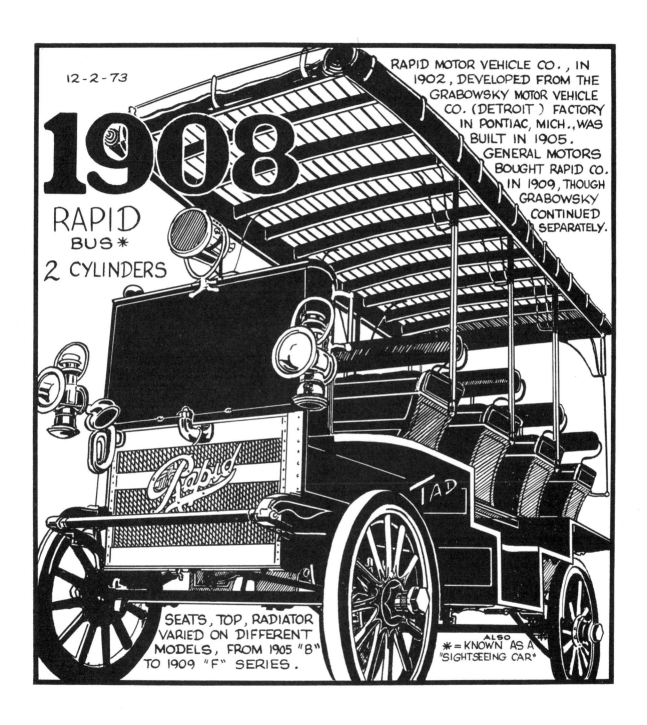

12-2-73

1908

RAPID
BUS *
2 CYLINDERS

RAPID MOTOR VEHICLE CO., IN 1902, DEVELOPED FROM THE GRABOWSKY MOTOR VEHICLE CO. (DETROIT) FACTORY IN PONTIAC, MICH., WAS BUILT IN 1905. GENERAL MOTORS BOUGHT RAPID CO. IN 1909, THOUGH GRABOWSKY CONTINUED SEPARATELY.

SEATS, TOP, RADIATOR VARIED ON DIFFERENT MODELS, FROM 1905 "B" TO 1909 "F" SERIES.

ALSO
* = KNOWN AS A "SIGHTSEEING CAR"

The years from 1910 to 1919 saw the rise of the Model T Ford, which became the sales leader among all cars. It seems that Henry Ford could not build them fast enough to meet the growing demand, even though by 1914 Model Ts were being mass-produced on assembly lines.

Beginning in Europe in 1914, World War I (then known as the Great War) involved America three years later. When the Armistice was signed and peace restored in November 1918, much of France and Western Europe lay in ruins. Automobile production in the United States did not stop during the war, as it did in World War II, but there were wartime shortages and rationing, and auto advertisements warned buyers to act promptly while they could still get a new car.

This period marked an evolution in automobile design, a change from the awkward "horseless carriage" of 1910 to the sleek, sophisticated touring car of 1919. The tires were still inferior; blowouts and punctures were frequent.

Lighter-than-air balloons had been around for years, but the airplane was still in its infancy a few years after Wilbur and Orville Wright's experimental 1903 flight at Kitty Hawk, North Carolina.

International travel was done by rail to neighboring countries and by ocean liner from continent to continent. Sea travel was marred by two disasters: the loss of the supposedly unsinkable *Titanic* in 1912, after a collision with an iceberg off Newfoundland; and the wartime torpedoing and sinking of the *Lusitania* in 1915, near Ireland. The death toll was high in each incident.

William H. Taft's Republican administration ended on Inauguration Day, March 4, 1913, when the Democrat Woodrow Wilson took office. Wilson hoped to avoid becoming embroiled in the new European conflict and was reelected in 1916 because "he kept us out of war," but in 1917 the United States went to the aid of its allies overseas. This swung the tide against the German kaiser, and "the war to end all wars" ended late the following year.

On the home front, the phonograph was a popular medium of entertainment. Songs reflecting the times included: "Heaven Will Protect the Working Girl" (1910), "Put Your Arms Around Me, Honey" (1910), "Alexander's Ragtime Band" (1911), "Oceana Roll" (1911), "On Moonlight Bay" (1912), "He'd Have to Get Under, Get Out and Get Under, to Fix Up His Automobile" (1913), "The International Rag" (1914), "Gasoline Gus and His Jitney Bus" (1915), "I Didn't Raise My Boy to Be a Soldier" (1915), "Poor Butterfly" (1916), "Over There" (1917), "Smiles" (1917), "Just a Baby's Prayer at Twilight (For Her Daddy Over There)" (1918), "K-K-K-Katy" (1918), "How Ya Gonna Keep 'Em Down on the Farm, After They've Seen Paree?" (1919), and "Take Your Girlie to the Movies" (1919).

A Time of Change

The 1910s

1910 Ford Model T

A 1910 advertisement for the Model T reads: "The same old Ford Motor Company has been manufacturing Ford cars designed by Henry Ford, since the very earliest days of the industry. The first automobile ever seen in Detroit was a Ford; one of the first half dozen built in America was designed and built by Ford; 40,000 Ford cars have since been built and all have made good. There never was a Ford failure — there never was an unfulfilled Ford promise, and the years have built up a reputation for Ford that it would be folly to risk at this late date (1910)."

The advertisement went on to relate how other, inferior, products enjoyed short-lived success in spite of heavy advertising, and that Ford's factory output had doubled each year since 1903, when the Ford Motor Company was officially founded. Ford cars were bought, the ad said, not because they were low priced but because they were *good*. A buyer could *depend* on them.

In addition to open cars, Ford also sold two closed models in 1910 — a coupe for $1050 and a town car for $1200 — which were suitable for bad weather. But for only $125 more Ford would sell the buyer of the closed car a supplementary touring car body, which could be installed on the coupe or town car chassis for use in warm weather. Changing bodies on a car seems terribly complicated and impractical today, but amazingly, the Ford advertisement of January 1, 1910, in the *Saturday Evening Post*, assured that the bodies could be interchanged in only one hour.

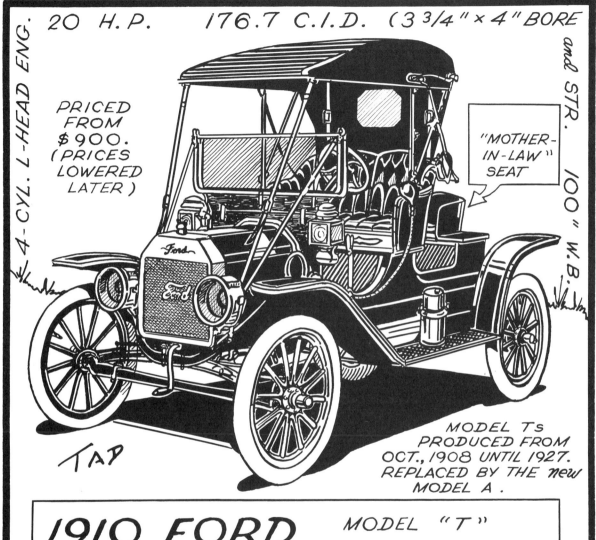

1911 Reeves Octoauto

Elbert Hubbard, the famous author who lost his life when the steamship *Lusitania* was torpedoed and sunk, wrote a convincing advertisement for the 1911 Reeves Octoauto under his own byline. He said that, years before, he had made several train trips to the Chicago stockyards to deliver cattle, and that on these trips he had usually traveled in the caboose. The standard eight-wheeled cabooses were comfortable enough, but occasionally a four-wheeled "dinkey" was substituted. A ride in a dinkey, related Hubbard, was the height of discomfort, for it would "bounce, jolt, jar and jerk, and make a puncture in your vocabulary."

Hubbard suggested that the same multiwheel principle that made for added comfort in both the railroad caboose and a Pullman car would also work in automobiles. Not only did the Octoauto give a luxurious, level ride, but the life of the car was prolonged by the even distribution of wear and tear over eight wheels rather than four. Also, no one corner of the car had to bear a full fourth of the load, as on ordinary cars.

The Octoauto received considerable attention but did not attract a rush of would-be buyers. It was followed by a six-wheeled Sexto-Auto, which had four wheels at the rear but only the usual two in front. Ultimately, these multiwheeled cars were unsuccessful. Milton Reeves had manufactured Motocycle cars in the late 1890s, and then a series of Reeves and Go-Buggy cars as well as air-cooled and water-cooled Reeves engines, which were sold in quantity to other auto manufacturers before 1910. Yet the multiwheeled cars are what Reeves is best remembered for today.

9-6-70

THANKS TO
F. C. WHITTINGTON,
COLUMBUS, IND.
FOR PHOTOS.

← TYPICAL HOUSE
OF 1911.

BUILT IN
COLUMBUS, IND.
BY REEVES
PULLEY CO.

TAR

1911 REEVES "OCTOAUTO"

4 CYLINDERS   40 H.P.   180-INCH WHEELBASE

EIGHT WHEELS, IT WAS BELIEVED, WOULD PROVIDE UNEQUALED RIDING COMFORT AND ADD TO TIRE LIFE. SIX WHEELS COULD BE STEERED. OVERLAND PARTS WERE USED. A 6-WHEELED "SEXTOAUTO" WAS ALSO EXPERIMENTAL, BUT NEITHER IDEA WAS SUCCESSFUL. STILL, THE OCTOAUTO IS ONE OF THE MOST FAMOUS OF ALL "FREAK" CARS... THE "BRAINCHILD" OF MILTON O. REEVES.   PRICE-$3200.00

1912 Alldays & Onions

The staid British owners of these picturesque little cars may have been self-conscious about their peculiar name. Some of them were referred to simply as Alldays.

The Alldays & Onions was famous in the British Empire in the days before World War I. Undoubtedly, most Americans have never heard of this one, and many will surely chuckle at the name, which sounds like something only a breath mint could remedy!

Not only were small models offered; there were also larger types, with four-cylinder and six-cylinder engines. The 30–35-horsepower limousine, for example, was a hefty piece of machinery with a towering, coachlike body and a very long hood (or bonnet, as the British say).

Alldays & Onions acquired the Enfield Autocar Company in 1908, and after 1918 the name of their combined product was changed to Enfield-Allday (without the final s on Allday).

Alldays & Onions cars are understandably scarce these days, but there's a 1904 model at the British National Motor Museum in Beaulieu, and a 1912 model exactly like the one shown here was offered for sale in 1968 by a noted antique auto dealer in England. There are probably just a few others remaining, scattered throughout the world.

1912

ALLDAYS & ONIONS

"MIDGET" MODEL
2-CYLINDER
L-HEAD
ENGINE
10/12 H.P.

BY ALLDAYS AND ONIONS PNEUMATIC ENGINEERING CO., LTD., BIRMINGHAM, ENGLAND (1898 - 1918)

ANCESTOR OF THE ENFIELD - ALLDAY CAR OF 1919 TO 1925.

TAD

9-14-75

What a name! BUT THERE WERE OTHER CARS WITH ODD NAMES, SUCH AS THE 7 LITTLE BUFFALOES (U.S.); PIPE (BELGIAN); "Z" (CZECH.); PIC-PIC; POPP (SWISS); ANGER; STEEL SWALLOW (U.S.); RUMPF (BELGIAN); AUTO-BUG; O-WE GO (U.S.); OLD MILL (BRITISH); KORN ET LATIL (FRENCH); KLEINSCHNITTGER (GERMAN); HYSLOP; KLINK (U.S.); GURGEL (BRAZILIAN); BAT; BEAN; COTTON (BRITISH)

1913 Garford

Why did Willys-Overland's Garford Six for 1913 offer the single headlight? (Some may remember the 1915 Briscoe touring car. It, too, had a single center headlight, though such an unusual feature was unacceptable to the public.)

To quote from various advertisements of 1913: "The Garford Six is the only automobile made with the headlight where it should be — in the center of the radiator. This new Garford method of lighting throws a flood of light directly on the road where it belongs. It is just as unnecessary to have two headlights on an automobile as it would be to have two on a locomotive."

Another ad proclaimed: "This new method of lighting eliminates the rattling, cumbersome and unsightly headlights that were always in the way. It gives the car a much cleaner and much more finished appearance." In this April 1913 Garford ad, the four people were placed almost as they are shown here, with the owner of the car using a stick to point out the unusual center light.

Garford (which once built chassis for Studebaker before Willys-Overland acquired the Garford Company) "had a thing with" unusual lights during 1913. In addition to the center light, its new model also had two "powerful bullseye electric lights" sunk flush with the cowl front as well as two concealed electric lights that illuminated the dash. Further, there was a "brilliant electric dome light" for the tonneau section (the so-called dome light being attached to the rear of the front seat).

The body was unusual on the touring car in that it was of all-steel "Pullman" construction in an era when most automobile bodies relied heavily on wood for inner support. But the center-headlight Garford was considered a white elephant at resale time, so very few survived.

Such a car, if found, would be a real treasure to any collector today.

1914 Packard 6

"Boss of the road!" Here's a magnificent old-timer that could qualify as both antique and classic.

Packard had introduced its first six-cylinder model during 1911 (for the 1912 season), and soon two series of sixes were offered: "48" and "38." (The Packard fours had been eliminated in 1913.)

Earlier "48" sixes had an engine with cylinders cast in three sets of two, but the 1914 model was described as having cylinders cast in threes, as on the "38."

This mighty "48" had a one-man top, a clock, Packard-Bijur electrical lighting and starting, and a power pump for inflating tires. For luxury, this Packard was equaled only by the new twelve-cylinder (V-12) Twin Six, introduced in 1915 (for 1916).

And what is a 1914 Packard worth these days? Well, some years ago, a fully restored specimen was advertised for $80,000, and since then the prices of most antique cars have increased.

Were antique cars ever cheap? Yes, in the 1930s the few cars from before World War I that could still run were considered unwanted, outdated old "dogs" and could be obtained at rock-bottom bargain prices. In 1932, my older cousin could have bought a 1916 Buick coupe for *seven dollars*. And in 1952, I was able to obtain a 1929 De Soto roadster, which ran well, for only $10! And I was satisfied in 1956 to sell it for $50, though it would be worth many times that amount today.

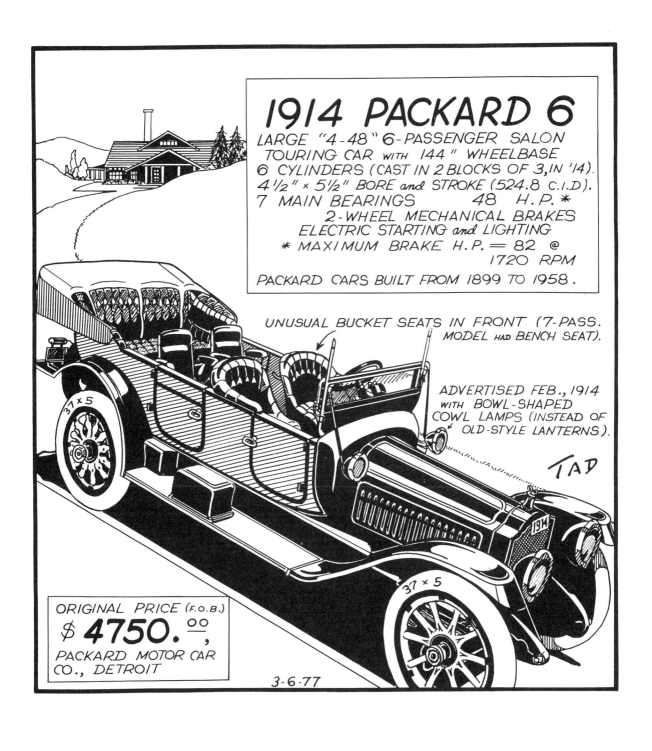

1914 Richmond

Popular auto references frequently list the earliest Richmond car as a 1908, but the 1914 Richmond catalogue claims the first Richmond car was produced in 1902. (It's possible the 1902 car was merely experimental, however.)

Unlike many discontinued "orphan" cars, the Richmond was built mainly of parts produced by its own manufacturer, the Wayne Works. The giant factory produced engines, transmissions, axles, bodies, tops, frames, steering gears, fenders, and so on.

Earlier, Richmond had built a sporty little Bumblebee roadster that featured a handy trunk in the rear deck. Also, there were two cars named Wayne. One was made in Richmond, Indiana, by the Wayne Works, but the better-known Wayne was built in Detroit.

The Richmond was guaranteed for ninety days after the date of shipment. But the warranty was void if the car should be altered or repaired "outside of our factory" within that period.

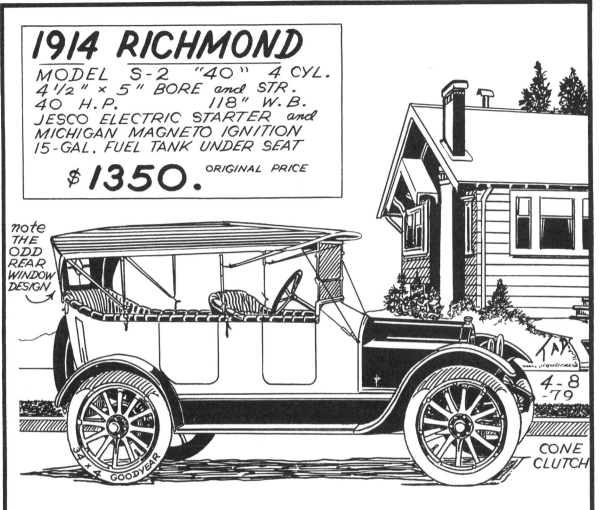

1915 Chevrolet Royal Mail Roadster

Here's a Chevy so old it wasn't even a General Motors product, for Chevrolet did not become a member of the GM family until 1918.

The Series H four-cylinder Chevrolet, beginning as a 1914 model, was the first four-cylinder Chevrolet and also the first with the characteristic overhead-valve engine. (Early six-cylinder Chevrolets used T-head and L-head engines.)

The earliest Royal Mail roadsters did not offer a self-starter as standard equipment (as did the early six), and the early crank-started models also featured gas lamps.

In 1915, the wheelbase was extended from 104 to 106 inches, and a starter was included as standard equipment (along with electric lights, as shown here).

Another new 1915 Chevrolet model was the sporting Amesbury Special roadster with its deluxe (and more modern) body, a folding one-piece windshield, and a lockable, watertight rear deck.

Wire wheels were available, and the Amesbury was finished entirely in French gray with nickel-plated brightwork.

The Royal Mail roadster and Baby Grand touring car were soon joined by a more popular new series: the Chevrolet "490." The model number referred to the initial price.

Because of Chevrolet's high popularity since the 1930s, it is surprising to discover that in 1921 a GM executive called the future of the Chevrolet "hopeless." That rash statement was to be proved wrong within a half-dozen years.

CHEVROLET

Royal Mail

ROADSTER   H-2

1915

$750⁰⁰

20 - GALLON FUEL TANK

4 CYL. O.H.V.
170.9 CID ENGINE
24 H.P.
3 11/16" x 4" B + ST.
new 106" WB.
'14 MODEL had DRUM
GAS HEADLIGHTS and
LG. COWL LANTERNS;
'16 MODEL had new
SLOPING "TURTLEBACK"
REAR DECK.

32 × 3½

32 × 3½

4 - DR. TOURING CAR (PHAETON) WAS "BABY GRAND" MODEL.

TAP
7-22
-79

1916 Dunn Cyclecar

Since this is a tiny four-cylinder vintage machine, I almost labeled it the Dunn 4. But that would be too obvious a pun, as the car was truly "done for," being discontinued within two years.

You may be astonished to notice the long list of seventy other makes of cyclecars. (There was room only for the A to J makes.)

The cyclecar craze was at its height around 1915; many cyclecars were considerably smaller — and much lighter — than today's subcompact cars. They were popular not only because they saved on gasoline (some had only two cylinders) but also because they were low priced and easy to drive.

Characteristic of these little vehicles are the narrow, lightweight wire wheels (many of the motorcyle or bicycle type). Some cyclecars, like this Dunn, had air-cooled engines, thus eliminating the added weight of a radiator. Some had detachable tops and windshields. Even Ford built an experimental cyclecar, somewhat like a miniature Model T.

But the cyclecars did not continue into the 1920s. For one thing, their steering systems left much to be desired. Many had simple rope-and-pulley steering, such as on a soapbox derby racer. Many had crude, weak brakes.

Furthermore, the highways were getting crowded after World War I, and flimsy little cars didn't stand a chance in a collision. Yet, if a safer cyclecar could be produced today, it might possess a definite appeal, especially from the standpoint of economy.

1916 DUNN

CYCLECAR (DUNN MOTOR WORKS, OGDENSBURG, N.Y. (1914-1918)

ALPHABETICAL LIST OF OTHER
CYCLE CARS (A-J ONLY!)

AJAX, AMERICAN, ARGO, ARROW,
AUTOCYCLE, AUTOETTE, AUTO TRI-CAR,
BANTAM, BEISEL, BROOKE-SPACKE,
BROWN, BUCKLES, BURROWS, B-Z-T,
CALIFORNIA, CAR-NATION, CECO
CHATAQUA, CHELSEA, CHICAGO,
COEY "BEAR," COLUMBIA, COMET,
CONTINENTAL, CORNELIAN, COTAY,
CRICKET, CROWN, CROXTON, CUB,
CYCLEMOBILE, CYCLEPLANE, DART,
DAVIS, DAYTON, DE CROSS, DETROIT,
DIAMOND, DOWNING, DRIGGS-SEABURY,
DUDLY "BUG," DUMORE, DUM,
DURYEA, EAGLE, EAGLE-MACOMBER,
ECONOMY, ECONOMYCAR, E.I.M.,
ELBERT, ENGLER, EUCLID, EXCEL,
FALCON, FAUBER AUTO CYCLE CAR,
FAULTLESS, FEDELIA, FENTON,
FLAGLER, FREDERICKSON,
GADABOUT, GRAY, GREYHOUND,
HALL, HANOVER, HAWK,
HOOSIER SCOUT,
IDEAL, IMP,
J.P.L.

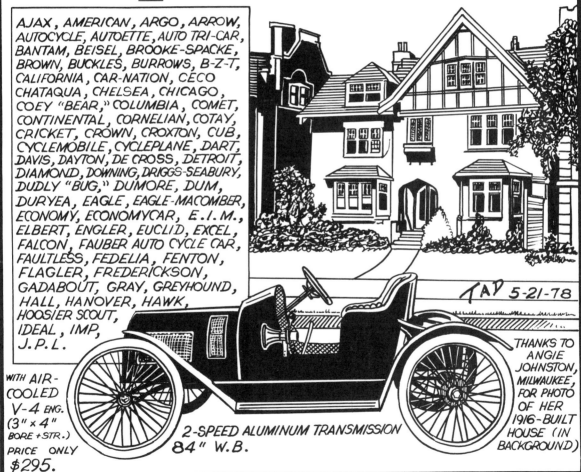

TAP 5-21-78

WITH AIR-
COOLED
V-4 ENG.
(3" x 4"
BORE + STR.)
PRICE ONLY
$295.

2-SPEED ALUMINUM TRANSMISSION
84" W.B.

THANKS TO
ANGIE
JOHNSTON,
MILWAUKEE,
FOR PHOTO
OF HER
1916-BUILT
HOUSE (IN
BACKGROUND)

1916½ Milburn Light Electric

It is reported that President Woodrow Wilson's Secret Service men used Milburn electric cars. That does seem strange; after all, an early electric car such as this would not even reach a top speed of 25 miles an hour. Hardly suitable for fast pursuit, you might think — unless one were chasing pedestrians. But for routine business in and around metropolitan Washington, D.C., an electric car was practical, as long as its batteries were recharged after a few hours' use.

Electric cars were well liked by ladies, as electrics were quiet, clean, and simple to drive.

"Never a bit of trouble," many owners reported of their Milburn Electrics.

Because of its light weight, the Milburn was easy on tires.

During 1916, twice as many Milburns were sold as were bought in their first full year of 1915.

Milburns were available with wood wheels as well as with the wire wheels shown here. And a few Milburns were fitted with outside visors, though in most of the advertisements of 1916–1917, no visor is shown. The ads frequently pictured the Milburn in various pastel hues, but Milburn blue and black were standard unless the buyer expressed another color choice.

Until the early 1920s, there were several brands of electric cars on the market.

1919 Auburn Beauty-Six

Most of the Auburn cars that exist today are from the Cord years, when E. L. Cord had control of the company and pushed it ahead, financially, through the mid-twenties and into the thirties.

Also, there are a limited number of beautiful new V-8-powered replicas of the 1936 Auburn speedsters (and phaetons) currently available.

Auburns, both new and old, are frequently seen at major car shows and auctions, not only throughout the United States but around the world. Yet how many car buffs have ever seen the rare, earlier type of Auburn such as this 1919 Beauty-Six?

This was, in general, similar to the type of car Auburn was building in 1924, when the company was in trouble and called on E. L. Cord to take charge and revitalize operations. As Auburn gained in popularity after that, the earlier models were nearly forgotten. And so we refresh the memory of those who may have seen a Beauty-Six many years ago.

Also, we include a list of popular song hits from the year this car was built. Some of the songs have retained their popularity, but others, like the elusive Beauty-Six, have faded into obscurity. Like this car, they are familiar only to antique collectors.

1919 Pan

The 1919 Pan was heralded as the "Pan Features Car of the Future." Looking fairly ordinary except for its running boards, which turned up at either end to join the fenders, the Pan nevertheless had new features not found elsewhere. The most salient feature was convertible seats, which folded to make a bed. Years later (1931), the Durant had seatbeds; and starting in 1936, Nash made them a strong selling point in its car for many years. But when the first Pan was revealed in 1918, a seatbed was an amazing novelty.

Another unusual idea was the combination compartment tank at the rear, which provided separate sections for food, ice, water, oil, tools, and a reserve supply of gasoline (the main fuel tank was in the cowl). The reserve supplies of gas, oil, and water could be tapped by the use of spigots attached below the reservoirs.

The headlights could be swiveled to use either as spotlights or as "trouble lights" to illuminate the engine and under the hood.

Samuel Conner Pandolfo, the founder and most exuberant promoter of the Pan Motor Company, wanted to get going in a big way with his new motor empire. Not only did he replace the original, low-cost Continental engine with an engine designed exclusively for his cars by Victor Gauvreau, a French engineer of considerable fame, but Pandolfo also built his own company town near St. Cloud, Minnesota, to house his employees. This was called Pan Town, and more than fifty houses were built at the start. There was also a Motor Hotel for visitors and bachelor employees, and a luxurious $30,000 home for Pandolfo himself.

Samuel Pandolfo's unusual stock schemes are said to have brought down the enterprise. A buyer of only $10 worth of Pan Motor stock was promised a $187.50 discount on the future purchase of a $1250 Pan automobile. This was a real bargain, but certain observers made haste to show that Pan's stock sales were far exceeding its auto production. As a result of such unfavorable publicity, Pandolfo was soon denied the license to sell stock in many states (including Minnesota) and was up to his ears in a long legal battle.

Appealing to the courts, he gained some time. But in 1922 the factory was closed for good and Pandolfo was jailed. In 1926 he opened a health food business in St. Cloud. Later he tried real estate, and eventually he returned to the insurance business, his original line of endeavor. Pandolfo died in 1960 at the age of eighty-four.

During the 1920s, the closed sedan became the most popular auto body type, displacing the open touring car. Hudson and Essex led the way in 1922 in making closed cars popular by pricing them down in the open-car range. Before 1925, more open than closed cars were sold. But after 1925, the trend reversed, as closed cars were now priced within the reach of all.

In the truck field, the Reo Speed Wagon was a leader, because it replaced the cumbersome, slow, solid-tired, low-geared "antique" truck with a modern "speed" type, which had the nimble, peppy performance of a car!

Italy's Lancia Lambda was a pioneer in new features and sports car performance, completely unlike the average car of the period.

The 1920s were a time of escalating prosperity and postwar expansion, though a business recession in 1920–1921 threatened at first to spoil the party. It was a foretaste of trouble to come.

America's suburbs grew as more families were liberated from the bounds of city transit systems by their new autos. In the vicinity of Los Angeles, for example, rural meadows and sunny acres of orange groves were sold, subdivided, and built up into suburban home tracts for miles and miles, as far as the eye could see. This booming expansion happened around many other cities as well. The one-story frame or stucco "bungalow" was the most popular kind of dwelling, usually with a low-pitched roof, wide front porch, and separate one-car garage at the rear of the lot.

After the 1920 elections (the first to be heard on radio), President Wilson's Democratic administration ended in March 1921, with Republican Warren G. Harding's inauguration. Upon Harding's death in 1923, Vice President Calvin Coolidge gained the presidency. Coolidge maintained a brief period of stable prosperity, but he did not choose to run for reelection in 1928 and was succeeded by Herbert Hoover. In October 1929, the wild manipulations and gambles of the stock market ended in a sudden crash, followed by the Great Depression of the early 1930s.

In the entertainment field, silent movies prevailed in the early and middle twenties, but in 1927 came Al Jolson's musical *The Jazz Singer*, which included talking and singing sequences and a good background musical score. In 1928 and 1929 came additional "talkies," and in 1929 there was a varied assortment of all-talking, all-singing musical films such as *Broadway Melody, The Cocoanuts, Fox Movietone Follies of 1929, Gold Diggers of Broadway, Hallelujah, Hollywood Revue of 1929, The Love Parade, On with the Show, Say It with Songs, Show of Shows, Sunny Side Up,* and *The Vagabond Lover,* starring the new singing and bandleading sensation, Rudy Vallee. After 1927, many popular tunes of the day were introduced in films.

Popular songs of the "roaring twenties" include such all-time hits as "Margie" (1920), "Ain't We Got Fun" (1921), "Whispering" (1921), "Toot, Toot, Tootsie" (1922), "Kitten on the Keys" (1922), "Yes, We Have No Bananas" (1923), "It Ain't Gonna Rain No More" (1924), "I'm Sitting on Top of the World" (1925), "Show Me the Way to Go Home" (1926), "My Blue Heaven" (1927), "I'll Get By" (1928), "Sonny Boy" (1928), "Ain't Misbehavin'" (1929), and "Broadway Melody" (1929).

We should also recall the great Florida land boom of the mid-twenties. It seemed that everyone "discovered" Florida at once, and there was an almost hysterical rush to buy and build in that sunny southland. Song hits were written about this phenomenon in 1925, such as "Florida," "Miami," and "Tamiami Trail," not to mention others. And the Marx Brothers starred in a zany stage musical, *The Cocoanuts,* in which Groucho was a wisecracking Florida resort manager who peddled lots on the side. The Marxes remade it as a movie for Paramount in 1929.

Boom and Bust

The 1920s

1920 Velie 48

During the late summer of 1919, Velie introduced its new 1920 Model 48, designed to create a new styling sensation.

This touring car and other 48s had a straight-line, high-cowl body, with squared-off corners replacing the usual compound curves. Velie called this "the first authoritative example of the new style," with "a subtle combination of mirror-like planes that seem to flow into each other."

In a day when so many touring cars looked virtually alike, the new Velie was a bold adventure in styling: a deliberate look of boxiness when curves were more in fashion. Even the shape of the windshield was unique, following the angular cowl.

In addition to five- and seven-passenger touring cars and other body types, there was also a four-passenger Tourster, with a jauntily sloping rear deck and a spare tire mounted parallel to it.

The Model 48, available in 1920 and 1921, was capable of speeds of up to 60 miles per hour. The improved six-cylinder engine of 1920 had larger valves as well as an internally heated vaporizer capable of burning low-grade fuel and giving greater gas mileage.

As 1920 began, Velie also introduced a lower-priced, smaller Model 34 that was more conventional in appearance. But it was this distinctive 48 that got most of the stares along the highway. It was almost an expression of Art Nouveau on wheels.

1921 Reo Speed Wagon

Today's antique car collectors often restore "depot hacks." Predecessors of today's station wagon, these were often a combination of open-sided station wagon and full-length covered pickup truck, all in one. There are, of course, variations.

The Reo Speed Wagon is correctly known as a "canopy express." It strongly resembles a depot hack, but a canopy express typically provides passenger seating only in the front seat while the covered rear section is reserved for freight.

When the Reo canopy express Speed Wagon appeared in 1915 (for the following season), it was several years ahead of its time, with electric lights, a self-starter, and pneumatic (air-filled) tires.

Most trucks of 1915 were slow, ponderous monsters that rode on bone-shaking solid tires and seldom exceeded 18 miles per hour (if they could get up that much speed). But the Reo Speed Wagon paved the way for a flood of various competitors' light "speed trucks," many of which appeared during the early 1920s.

(We should not overlook the cute little Vim truck, a stubby-looking but appealing canopy express that appeared in the mid-teens.)

By September 1920, more than forty thousand Reo Speed Wagons were in service — twice the number reported in May 1919.

Farmers and business people were urged, in ads, to "Standardize on Reos," because Reo offered a full line of passenger cars in addition to these other Speed Wagon types of 1921: Convertible Carry-All (depot hack style, $1600), Ideal Dairy Truck (pickup, $1575), Grain Box (with attached, high solid sides, $1625), Stock Rack (a pickup with high slat sides, $1600), and Truck Farmers' Double Deck Van ($1600 — like the model illustrated, but with an extra deck for added capacity).

1922 Gearless Steamer

"Pittsburgh's Superior Motor Cars," read the original sales folder for the Gearless Steamer. Notwithstanding its name, the car was not entirely gearless: there were small cogs in the engine. But it had no transmission (hence "Gearless"). The steam engine (shown upright, for clarity) was actually mounted in a horizontal position under the floor of the car, with the crankshaft aligned with the rear wheels, for direct drive. Under the hood was the boiler — also the condenser.

The Gearless carried twenty gallons of fuel (such as kerosene) plus twenty-five gallons of water, which was boiled for motive power. Also, eight quarts of oil provided lubrication (which was not very complete, since so many moving parts were exposed).

Only a few roadsters and touring cars are known to have been actually built, though sedans were promised. The Gearless Company skidded toward oblivion after its four principal officers were indicted by a federal grand jury for using the mails to defraud and for conspiracy. Much stock had been sold, but too few cars had been produced to please detractors. One disgruntled dealer touched off the company panic by suing the manufacturer when he failed to deliver the promised cars but tried to pacify him with a hundred shares of stock.

The Gearless looked not unlike the Stanley or the Doble, the two leading steamers of their day. But the market for steam cars was a very limited one, especially by the 1920s, and the Gearless people just didn't have the will or the wherewithal to get their act fully together.

As many as eight Gearless Steamers (or perhaps other cars posing as such) have been shown together in one photograph. But just try to locate *one* of these extremely rare cars today!!

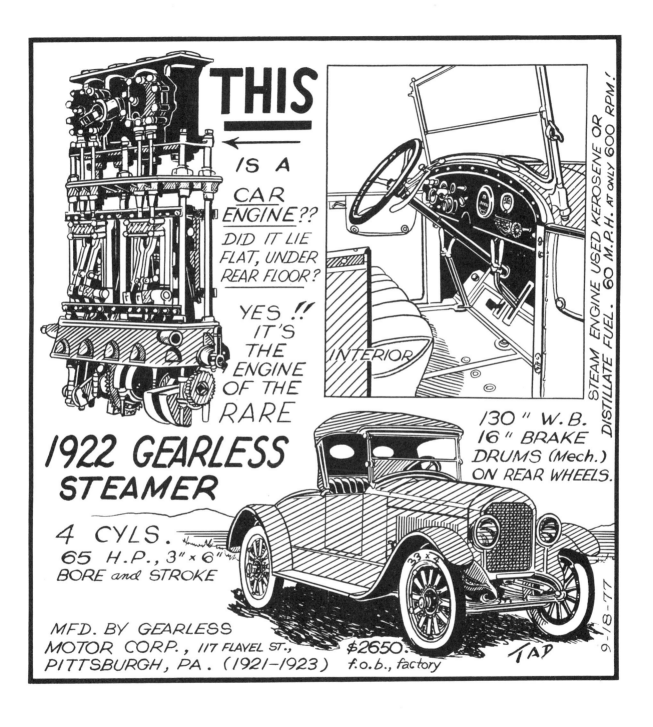

1922 Scripps-Booth

Some readers may remember the peculiar-looking 1913 Bi-Auto-Go. Half motorcycle, half car, it was the first of a line of Scripps-Booth vehicles. Next came a small cyclecar, then a full-sized line of lightweight models, most of which sported wire wheels.

The final Scripps-Booth products included this 1922 Medium Weight Six roadster as well as a touring car, a four-door sedan, and a four-passenger coupe.

The 1922 roadster bodies were painted dark blue or maroon, with black fenders and chassis aprons. The upholstery was of genuine long-grain dull black leather in the open models. (Closed cars were upholstered in "wool coach cloth.")

Open-car tops were of genuine Pantasote, fully lined. The oblong rear window was fitted with bevel-edge plate glass. Tools were carried in the left front door.

All the models had a lighting and ignition switch with a key lock. "So what?" you may say. But though today we take ignition locks for granted, many early autos had nonlocking ignition switches and could be easily stolen by so-called joy riders.

One feature, though, that even many later cars did not possess was the stationary motor light, located under the hood. It certainly came in handy when there were mechanical problems after dark and no flashlight was available.

1922 SCRIPPS - BOOTH

"MEDIUM WEIGHT SIX" 3-PASS. ROADSTER (F-44)

$1470.

50-H.P., 6-CYL. L-HEAD CONTINENTAL ENGINE (3¼" × 4½") REPLACES THE SMALLER 40-H.P. 6 CYL. VALVE-IN-HEAD Northway ENGINE USED UNTIL 1921.

SCRIPPS-BOOTH, CO., DETROIT (1913-1922) (BOUGHT BY G.M. IN 1918.)

THESE FINAL MODELS DIDN'T HAVE A "VEE" RADIATOR

115" WB 15-GAL. FUEL TANK 32 × 4" CORD GOODYEAR TIRES

MANY THANKS TO KENNETH V. LOTTICK, SCOTTSDALE, ARIZONA, WHO PROVIDED ORIGINAL FACTORY LITERATURE ON THIS VERY RARE CAR!

2-5-78

1923 Packard Single Six

"How could a big old Packard like this get as much as eighteen to twenty miles a gallon?" you might ask in disbelief. It was true. Many Packard owners were reporting this surprising fuel economy with their Single Sixes.

And why was the six-cylinder Packard known as the *Single* Six? Because Packard had also manufactured, until 1923, a large V-12 that they proudly called the Twin Six; it was revived in 1932 and offered until 1939.

As for the 1923 Single Six, Packard announced it was their best seller yet. From November 1922, the Packard works were producing an average of over two thousand Single Sixes every six months!

One admirable feature of the Single Six was its precision crankshaft, riding in seven hefty main bearings, which was claimed to be vir-tually vibrationless. It took "55 precision machines" to produce each Packard crankshaft, the dimensions of which were checked with instruments "accurate to one ten-thousandth" of an inch.

Packards are most easily recognized by the shape of their radiators. This traditional shape was continued for years, even when radiators disappeared behind grilles in the early 1930s.

Then Packard incorporated the familiar fluted hood-and-grille combination into their yearly styling.

As in the case of the Lincoln, many old Packards were converted into tow trucks and pickups during the Depression because converting these reliable old machines was less expensive than purchasing new equipment.

TOURING CAR:

$2485.

6-8-80

1923 PACKARD *SERIES 126 "SINGLE SIX"*

WITH 268½ CID, L-HEAD 6-CYL. ENGINE   54 HORSEPOWER
(3⅜" × 5" BORE and STROKE)   33 × 4½ TIRES   4.33 GEAR RATIO
2-WHEEL MECHANICAL BRAKES   126" WHEELBASE
(V-12 "TWIN 6" REPLACED BY *new* STRAIGHT-8 LATER IN '23.)

MFD. BY PACKARD MOTOR CAR CO., DETROIT (1899-1958)

1924 Lancia Lambda

Long and lean as a praying mantis, this Lancia Lambda is unlike any other car ever built. Dramatically low to the ground in an era of high "top hat" autos, the Lambda was an amazing sensation when it was introduced late in 1922.

Though not intended as a sports car, the Lambda was soon adopted as one. Few European cars were brought into the United States before the late 1940s, but the Lancia Lambda was a rare exception. It found favor with the Hollywood set and with wealthy playboys who desired powerful and unusual automobiles.

The V-4 overhead-cam engine was unique, and a hot performer for its day. Few other cars could outrun this gazelle!

Its unitized body was also a new idea, nearly two generations ahead of its time. The body and frame were one, and the deep driveshaft tunnel on the floor was something unseen on other cars, which rode high on their separate chassis frames.

The Lancia Lambda is an easy car to recognize because of its low, long silhouette. The roadster, with its almost flat rear deck, looks even lower than this touring car and resembles a flattened Stutz Bearcat.

In its successful ten-year model run, the Lambda underwent only minor changes. Some closed models were built, with custom bodies available.

The Lambda was a work of art on wheels, and a milestone in automotive engineering. It's a masterpiece that will never be forgotten!

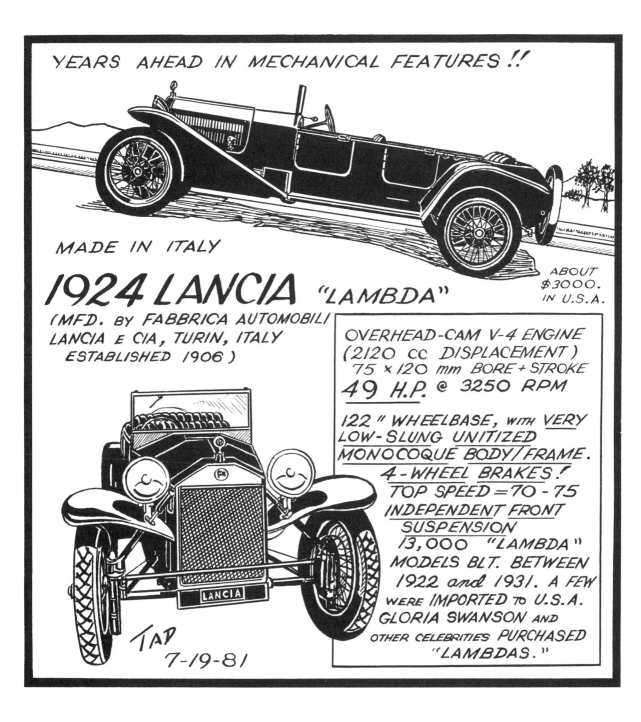

YEARS AHEAD IN MECHANICAL FEATURES !!

MADE IN ITALY

1924 LANCIA "LAMBDA"

ABOUT $3000. IN U.S.A.

(MFD. BY FABBRICA AUTOMOBILI LANCIA E CIA, TURIN, ITALY ESTABLISHED 1906)

OVERHEAD-CAM V-4 ENGINE (2120 CC DISPLACEMENT) 75 × 120 mm BORE + STROKE
49 H.P. @ 3250 RPM

122" WHEELBASE, WITH VERY LOW-SLUNG UNITIZED MONOCOQUE BODY/FRAME.
4-WHEEL BRAKES!
TOP SPEED = 70-75
INDEPENDENT FRONT SUSPENSION
13,000 "LAMBDA" MODELS BLT. BETWEEN 1922 and 1931. A FEW WERE IMPORTED TO U.S.A. GLORIA SWANSON AND OTHER CELEBRITIES PURCHASED "LAMBDAS."

LANCIA

TAD 7-19-81

1925½ Franklin

Until the early 1950s, there were quite a few Franklins from the late 1920s (known to historians as the "De Causse" Franklins) still in dependable service around the country (and, for that matter, throughout the world).

The De Causse Franklin of 1925½ to 1928 was a massive-looking machine but considerably lighter than it appeared because it rode on a *wooden* chassis frame. This light weight was also possible because the Franklin was air-cooled, thus eliminating all the extra equipment needed in the conventional, water-cooled engine (as well as the weight of the water itself).

Yes, that impressive radiator was a fake, but it did serve to admit fresh air to the blower fan. The radiator design, with its attractive vertical strips of brightwork, inspired some imitations. Chandler and Durant, for example, used vertical strips on their radiators not long after the De Causse Franklin appeared.

The De Causse model (series 11) replaced, in March 1925, the dated 10-C, which had a sloping, cathedral-shaped radiator somewhat like that of a Kissel.

In the Franklin engine, each cylinder was cast as a unit, with a series of vertical copper ribs. The cooling blower forced fresh air through a shroud, above the overhead-valve mechanism, and then vertically down past the cooling ribs.

Seven-window sedans were seen most frequently, but because of the unique shape of the early De Causse coupe, I just had to draw both body types for you to see. Also available (by July 1925) were a touring car, a sport runabout (roadster), an enclosed-drive limousine, a cabriolet, and a five-window sport sedan with landau irons and trunk.

1925 ½ SERIES 11
FRANKLIN
INTRODUCED MARCH, 1925

$3200.
(SEDAN) 3175 lbs.

2- WHEEL BRAKES (REAR)

all-new FRONT-END STYLING BY De Causse.

6 - CYL. AIR - COOLED engine (199.1 C.I.D., 3¼" × 4" BORE + STROKE)
33 HORSEPOWER @ 2200 RPM (4.4 COMPR.)

COUPÉ has UNUSUAL "CONTINENTAL" STYLE OF REAR DECK.

$2700.
2965 lbs.

TAD 7-27-75

4.73 GEAR RATIO

119" WHEELBASE

31 × 5.25 TIRES

1926 Checker Cab

A sixty-year era ended in 1982, when Checker production halted in Kalamazoo, Michigan, on July 12. For years a leader in taxi production, Checker had lost ground to De Soto in the late 1930s and the 1940s, when Chrysler Corporation's De Soto Division was supplying huge fleets of taxis to Yellow Cab and other major systems. In the 1950s, De Soto's cab production diminished, creating new opportunities for Checker. In 1959 Checker began to supplement its cab business with private, noncommercial automobiles (the Superba and Marathon models). Checker also built multidoored airport buses and high-topped Medicars (invalid transporters). During the late forties and early fifties they had also built about a thousand large city buses, similar in style to the more common GMC bus.

From the late fifties through the seventies, Checker was the preferred cab because of its roomy interior and high stance, which allowed easy entry and exit. In 1979, though, there was a downturn in the American auto industry, brought on by another round of manipulated price hikes and oil "shortages" from the Mideast. Increased foreign competition, union demands, and the need for energy efficiency cut deeply into Checker's business, and the small company lost $448,000 in 1981. Plans to launch a totally redesigned model for 1983 were shelved with the decision to curtail production.

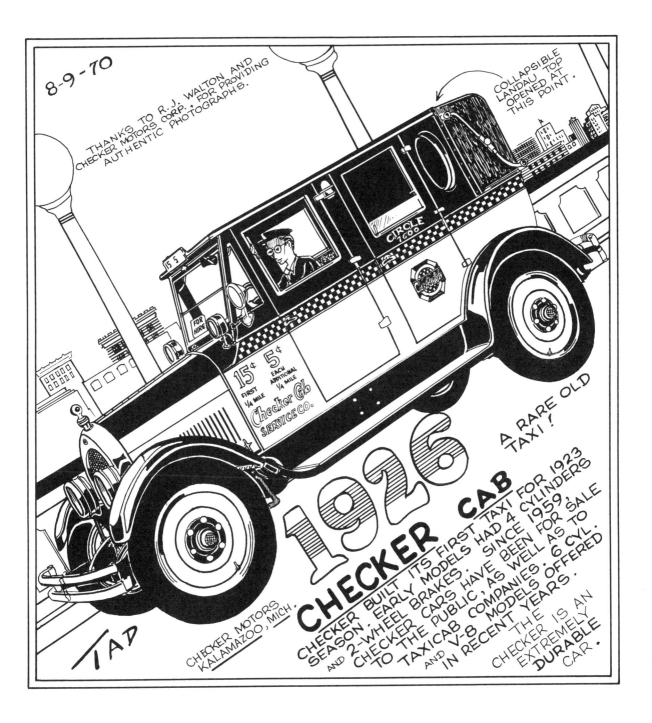

1927 Chrysler "60"

One of the most quaint of all vintage cars — and certainly scarce — is the Chrysler five-window coupe of the late twenties, which appeared in the light six-cylinder 1927 "60," 1928 "62," and 1929 "65" series. Most Chrysler coupes before the mid-1930s were three-window coupes (minus the extra side, or quarter, windows shown on this "60" coupe).

The "60" and "62" five-window rumble-seat coupes were low and solid looking, appearing to cling to the road like a bulldog; this feeling was enhanced by the comparatively small 18-inch wheels. The "60" and "62" looked alike except that the "62" had drum-type headlights instead of the bullet-shaped lights shown on this "60." Also, the "62" did not have cowl lamps (with rare exceptions) and had a new instrument panel with gauges framed separately on an oblong plate of attractive machine-turned metal.

The restyled "65" for 1929 had an instrument panel similar to that of the "62" it replaced, but the oblong plate was painted. The "65" had the new narrow-profile radiator found on Chryslers of 1929–1930, but a five-window rumble-seat coupe was still offered in addition to the more commonplace three-window business (trunk) coupe.

Early models of the "60" series (those built before 1927) had a much longer sun visor, which protruded more prominently. But the slightly overlapping roof with the stubby visor hung underneath was a feature of the late "60s," the "62s," the "65s," and also of some four-cylinder Chrysler "50," "52," and early Plymouth models. This roof-and-visor treatment was also seen on some Packards of the late twenties.

1927 Pierce-Arrow "36"

One hundred horsepower! That was a very high figure for any car back in 1927, but the mighty Pierce-Arrow Series 36 had a full 100 horsepower then. There were two Pierce-Arrow types at the time: the "36" and the 90-horsepower "80," which cost less and rode on a short (130-inch) wheelbase.

Pierce-Arrow prices ranged from $2895 to $8000 in 1927, but during the year the lowest-priced "80" became available for just $2495. The two model series can easily be distinguished from one another, since the "80" has, on each side of the hood, one long, continuous row of hood louvres while the illustrated "36" has six narrow groups of three louvres. On the big "36," the B.K. vacuum booster gave added power to the four-wheel mechanical brakes.

Established in 1901 in Buffalo, New York, the Pierce-Arrow Motor Car Company produced quality automobiles until 1938. During the later 1930s, Pierce-Arrow also turned out a small line of fine aluminum travel trailers.

In 1928, Studebaker took control of Pierce-Arrow for a few years, as they later did with Packard in the fifties. But Studebaker eventually gave Pierce-Arrow its independence again, though, by the mid-1930s, the Buffalo auto manufacturer was in extreme financial difficulty because there was such a small market remaining for its luxurious motorcars, which were built by an old-fashioned but meticulous handcrafted process.

1928 Studebaker Dictator 6

Studebaker introduced new model names for 1928. The former Standard 6 was renamed the Dictator 6. In addition, the Commander and President names (formerly certain body designations only) became new 1928 series that replaced the old Special 6 and Big 6. (The President for 1928 was Studebaker's first car with a straight-eight engine.)

Why did Studebaker pick the Dictator name? Dictators have never been highly regarded in the United States, but Studebaker officials believed that the name designated leadership, as did the other new model names. After 1937, however, the Dictator was "phased out" in an era when dictators were smothering human liberty.

Two stock Dictator sedans early in the 1928 season proved their mettle in an AAA-sponsored test run of twenty-four hours of continuous operation (average speed over 60). The advertisements of 1928 mentioned this as well as the good news that the new Dictator could be driven at 40 miles per hour when brand new, therefore eliminating the necessity of the customary long period of extra-slow, break-in speeds.

Moreover, lubrication and oil changes were said to be necessary for this car only every 2500 miles instead of at the traditional 1000-mile intervals.

During the latter half of 1928, new Studebakers with the more modern 1929 styling were on the market.

1929 Ford Model A

In the 1920s, Cantrell and other custom coach builders were supplying wooden station wagon bodies to auto manufacturers on an individual basis. But, in 1929, Ford became the first automaker to build its own station wagon bodies in regular factory production, and for some years Ford built more station wagons than any competitor.

The wooden station wagon was in style throughout the 1930s and 1940s, though General Motors began building metal-bodied wagons (Carryalls) on its GMC truck chassis in the mid-thirties.

The 1946 Jeep wagon and the 1949 Plymouth Suburban were the first popular all-steel station wagons. Many other 1949 and 1950 station wagons had bodies of steel, with wood used only for decorative trim outside. Within a few years, though, even the decorative wood gave way to imitation decals, and the later 1950s saw wooden body–making become a lost art.

A generation ago, any old wooden-bodied station wagon was laughingly called a woodpecker's delight. Things have changed, though. These days, vintage "woodies" command more respect!

1929 Whippet 4

In styling, the 1929 Whippet 4 was a far cry from its plain-looking predecessor. But the most unusual feature of the new car was the unique Finger Tip Control, a new type of horn button with many functions.

Power in the Whippet 4 engine was raised to 40 horsepower (formerly 31) because of an increase in compression and lengthening of rod stroke. Aluminum-alloy pistons and a "silent" timing chain were other engine advantages.

The 4 was distinguishable from the 6 in that it was shorter (a 103¼-inch wheelbase as compared to 112 for the 6); also, the 6 had cowl-mounted parking lamps seldom seen on the 4s.

The improved Whippet of 1929 was so good that it went virtually unchanged into 1930, and later that year the final "early '31" models continued. Yet the superior Whippet did not sell as well as the earlier models. Willys-Overland was having financial problems, and during early 1930, attention was focused on the all-new Willys six. (After all, a whippet is a *dog*.)

For several years before, cars bearing the Willys name had been Willys-Knights, with sleeve-valve Knight engines. But the Willys Six of 1930 offered a conventional side-valve L-head engine, which appealed to more people. So the Whippet was almost ignored in 1930 once the Willys Six was available. (There was also a Willys straight-eight.)

The Willys-Knight was dropped in 1933, the year that an all-new Willys "77" appeared. The "77" was a Spartanly simple and very low-priced small 4. It was suitable for the "threadbare thirties" and helped save Willys-Overland from becoming another bankrupt "orphan" company.

In the early 1930s, the Model A Ford was on the road in droves. It was much improved over the old Model T, and though discontinued in 1932, the Model A was a common sight on the highways a generation later.

And the Classic Era was here, with luxurious cars like Cadillac V-16s, Duesenbergs, Lincolns, Packards, Pierce-Arrows, and Chrysler Imperial Eights vying for sales among the fortunate few who could afford them.

As the thirties began, even the small, low-priced cars adopted the features of the big luxury ones, such as fender-mounted spare wheels, chrome-plated grilles or radiator screen guards, broadcloth upholstery, wire wheels, white sidewall tires, add-on trunks, elaborate radiator ornaments, fancy instrument panels, and the like.

The decade started with a long business depression. In many areas, more than 25 percent of the working population was unemployed, often with no public financial aid available. President Hoover was publicly lambasted for "not doing enough," for "siding with the wealthy," and for "being only for big business." He lost at the polls in 1932 to New York's Democratic governor, Franklin D. Roosevelt. FDR was also a rich man, but people saw him as more interested in the plight of the poor and middle-class citizens. After his inauguration in 1933 he expanded the role of the federal government to include many new social programs, agencies, and public works corps.

Residential architecture changed during the 1930s. Early in the decade, the most popular styles had been the low-roofed, boxy, white stucco Spanish or the half-timbered, high-roofed English Tudor; and wooden bungalows were usually made of closely lapped siding with low, composition-shingle or tar-and-gravel roofs, as in the 1920s. As the Depression deepened, home construction dwindled. In 1933 and 1934, for example, few new homes were built, and even in 1935 things were quite slow. In 1936 construction began to pick up, reflecting business in general. And in the later 1930s the most popular new house style by far was the low-roofed California ranch, which would typify the many sprawling tracts of the 1940s and 1950s.

Americans sought escape from their problems at the movies. Film stars and film companies prospered with the rise of stars such as Clark Gable, Gary Cooper, Joan Crawford, Bette Davis, Greta Garbo, and a youngster named Shirley Temple.

Radio also grew in popularity through the 1930s because it was free home entertainment. In popular music, the big new name was Bing Crosby, who rose to instant fame on radio and records in 1931, after spending a few years as one of Paul Whiteman's three Rhythm Boys. Another young popular "crooner" was Russ Columbo, from California, but his career was cut short in 1934 by a tragic gunshot accident. His aged mother was never informed of his death, and she continued to receive forged postcards and letters from "her son."

Among the song hits of the 1930s were: "Happy Days Are Here Again" (1930), "Walkin' My Baby Back Home" (1931), "Let's Have Another Cup of Coffee" (1932), "A Shanty in Old Shanty Town" (1932), "Love Is the Sweetest Thing" (1933), "Marching Along Together" (1933), "The Object of My Affection" (1934), "You Oughta Be in Pictures" (1934), "Lullaby of Broadway" (1935), "Pennies from Heaven" (1936), "The Merry-Go-Round Broke Down" (1937), "Thanks for the Memory" (1938), "Tip-Pi-Tin" (1938), "God Bless America" (1939), and "Over the Rainbow" (1939).

The Classic Years

The 1930s

1930 Cadillac V-16

The epitome of Cadillac's classic magnificence was reached during the early 1930s with the new V-16. In such lean times as those, it would seem to many today to have been the worst of taste — bordering on absolute cruelty — to drive a long, ostentatious, luxury automobile past lines of hungry, resentful people.

However, one should remember that the sixteen-cylinder Cadillac was conceived and developed during the prosperous boom years of the late 1920s, but it was not ready until 1930.

Many words have already been written about the sixteen-cylinder Cadillacs, which were available from 1930 to 1940. However, the V-16s from 1930 to 1937 had overhead-valve engines of 452 c.i.d., whereas the extremely rare 1938 to 1940 models had L-head engines, reduced to 431 c.i.d. The yearly production of the V-16s was usually well below five hundred. From 1934 to 1937, the V-16 Cadillac had an enormous wheelbase: 154 inches!

Cadillac production began in 1902, and a few years later, Cadillac joined the General Motors family. The early 1915 Cadillacs introduced their famous V-8 engine. In addition to the V-8 and V-16 models in the 1930s, there was also a V-12 (twelve-cylinder) Cadillac available from 1931 to 1937.

The V-16 was a superb car in every respect but performance; the sixteen cylinders provided smoothness but could in no way match the thunderous pep of the Duesenberg straight-eight J and SJ models of the thirties.

From 1931 to 1934, Marmon also produced a V-16 series. And Peerless built but one such car, in 1932.

1930 Dodge Eight

Available only in the early thirties, the straight-eight models of Dodge and De Soto are nearly forgotten now. Announced in the *Saturday Evening Post* of January 25, 1930, the Dodge Eight appeared shortly after the new $995 De Soto Eight, which had been announced three weeks earlier in the *Post*. New Chrysler straight-eights appeared in the summer of 1930, for the 1931 season.

Because the Dodge Eight came on the scene with an unproved new engine, a sedan of this model was later tested in a grueling Mileage Marathon, touring the country over the worst of roads and, in Utah, over miles of *railroad ties*. Before Christmas of 1930, the test car had covered sixty thousand miles in twenty-four weeks (since July 1).

The Chrysler straight-eight, a greater suc-

cess, was continued for two decades, through 1950, but the De Soto Eight was dropped during 1931, and the final Dodge Eight was the 1933 model. Sixes were preferred by Depression car buyers.

Eventually, overhead-valve V-8 engines became popular: Chrysler's V-8 coming for 1951, De Soto's for 1952, and Dodge's for 1953.

Plymouth, Chrysler Corporation's price leader for many years, never featured a straight-eight. But a Plymouth V-8 appeared for 1955.

Despite the angle at which the modern dash panel is shown, the gauges were symmetrical. In some Dodge Eights of 1930, the position of the speedometer and ignition lock were reversed, as in some other '30 Chrysler products.

1930 Hupmobile 8

"Hupmobile!" some readers may snort. "What a name! Was it for real?" It certainly was.

The first Hupmobile was the 1909 model and the final 1941 model was built in 1940. Now that the Hupp Motor Car Corporation has been out of business for some time, the name of the car may indeed evoke laughter from those who never heard of it before.

But Hupmobile was a popular name in the automotive world, especially during the 1920s and early 1930s, when Hupp introduced many desirable models, some with very dramatic styling.

This 1930 Model H is interesting because of its early modern "art deco" look. As the 1920s came to a dizzying and prosperous climax in 1929, there was a new flurry of interest in modernistic, streamlined styling.

Cars were still boxy in shape, but they could be embellished, as here, with decorative touches to give them an up-to-date look: such as in the design of the windshield, the instrument panel, the inside and outside door handles, the window frames, emblems, hubcaps, and upholstery patterns.

In one of its advertisements in 1930, Hupp presented a dramatic, glamorized head-on view of its new Model H, similar to this car, that emphasized the all-new styling touches.

This art deco type of design is said to have originated at the Paris International Exhibition of 1925, but its roots go back to the early years of this century and the Art Nouveau style.

Just another used jalopy fifty years ago, the 1930 Hupmobile H is now a rolling example of unusual artwork. (A seven-passenger model, on a 137-inch wheelbase, was called a Model U Hupmobile.)

1930 MODEL H — HUPMOBILE 8

133 HP
@ 3400 RPM
$1985 and up

365.6 CID
STRAIGHT-8 L-HEAD ENG.
125" WB

4.07 G.R.

12-9-79

TOP SPEED : 90
6.50 × 19 TIRES
MIDLAND MECHANICAL BRAKES

DASH ≡ "DECO-ART" STYLING ≡

OUTSIDE DOOR HANDLE

TAD

1930 Windsor 8

Near the end of the 1920s, the Moon Motor Car Company of St. Louis was in financial distress, as was Gardner, of the same city. For many years St. Louis had been a "little Detroit," with a few independent manufacturers turning out quality automobiles on a smaller scale than in the Motor City.

There was much competition and price cutting among the larger manufacturers during the twenties, with the result that many smaller companies suffered.

For 1929, the Moon people decided to add to their line a companion car, the Windsor. Further named White Prince and Royal in honor of the popular Edward, Prince of Wales, the 1929–1930 Windsor was attractive. Its radiator design was similar to the Moon's, but the hood louvres were horizontal. Automatic chassis oiling was offered.

During the course of 1929, Moon's corporate attention swung over to the new Windsor line. And so, for 1930, only the Windsor sixes and eights were available, with no new Moon model. Moon was also involved in an ill-fated deal with New Era Motors to coproduce, with Kissel, the new front-drive Ruxton car. Moon also merged its sales forces with Gardner.

The Ruxton car, with its low-slung, modernistic body and its peculiar, narrow Woodlite headlights, was a classic beauty but a commercial failure that contributed to the downfall of Moon, Gardner, and Kissel in the very early thirties.

Windsor's styling is less radical than Ruxton's, but the Windsor six- and eight-cylinder models were attractive, too. Many of the Ruxtons were recognized as potential classics and preserved, but fewer specimens remain of the Windsor or of the final Moon.

1931 American Rolls-Royce

Most people believe that the Rolls-Royce is a totally British car, and indeed it is — today. And it was — before 1920.

However, in 1920, because of the increasing popularity of the Rolls-Royce among wealthy American buyers, it was decided to assemble an American model at Springfield, Massachusetts. The resulting American Rolls-Royces were often larger and more ostentatious than their British counterparts.

But the American version was not continued after the early 1930s. Some wealthy buyers had the mistaken idea that everything imported was better and that, therefore, the quality of the American model was inferior to that of the British.

This was not true. Attention to fine detail and utmost quality was keen in both Rolls-Royce factories. Yet, some American buyers continued to order their new Rolls-Royces from England, ignoring the first-rate Massachusetts product.

When the Depression cut into Rolls-Royce's business everywhere, it was decided the continuation of the Springfield factory was sheer futility, so it was closed.

1931½ Graham Prosperity Six

In January 1931, Graham was offering a Standard 6 and Special 6, each with a 115-inch wheelbase and vertical hood louvres. Also available were two straight-eights, with vent doors along the hood: the Special 8, with a 120-inch wheelbase, and the Custom 8, with a hefty 134-inch wheelbase. Both the Special 6 and the eights had four-speed transmissions.

Then, in May 1931, Graham brought forth a new, lower-priced series. This was the Depression-born Prosperity Six, priced from only $785 (f.o.b. Detroit). Its wheelbase was 113 inches, and a three-speed transmission was used. The Prosperity Six resembled the other Graham sixes except that its fender-mounted parking lights were streamlined and built down into the fenders. Fender parking lights on the other models were set on little pedestals and resembled miniature headlights.

The Prosperity Six was introduced in four body types: a business coupe ($785); a rumble-seat coupe ($825); a five-window, four-door town sedan ($795); and a seven-window, four-door sedan ($825). Five or six wire wheels were available at extra cost, as was safety glass throughout.

In July, the Prosperity Six changed from a late 1931 to an early 1932 model as far as registration was concerned, and "free wheeling" was offered as an option. This low-priced Graham, unlike most other cut-rate models, offered most of the features found on the larger cars. It certainly did not look cheap, but when the streamlined Blue Streak Graham 8 appeared in 1932, all the preexisting Grahams seemed outdated.

'31½ (STARTS 5-10-31)

70 H.P. @ 3200 RPM
5.45 COMPR.

GRAAHAM

PROSPERITY SIX

TOWN SEDAN
$795.

(7-WINDOW SEDAN ALSO BUILT.)

6-CYL. L-HEAD 207 C.I.D. ENGINE
3⅛" x 4½" BORE and STR.

2176

5.00 x 19

4.45 GEAR RATIO (4.9 OPTIONAL)
12½-GALLON FUEL TANK

113" WHEELBASE
HYDRAULIC BRAKES (12" DRUMS)
COINCIDENTAL STEERING-and-IGNITION LOCK

TAD
2-1-76

1932 Essex Super 6

The "Pacemaker for 1932," this Essex was the final model of a marque begun in 1919 by the Hudson Motor Car Company of Detroit as a lower-priced subsidiary.

The 1932 Essex was loaded with features: a balanced crankshaft; synchro-mesh transmission with 50 miles an hour possible in silent second gear; a triple-sealed, oil-cushion clutch; labyrinthian oil cooling; power dome antiknock combustion chambers; Startix (an automatic self-starter and antistall device popular on many of the more expensive '32 cars); diagonal truss frame; twin "neutratone" mufflers; "ride control," free-wheeling; a "quick vision" instrument panel, with two large dark-faced dials and warning lights for oil and generator signals; arc-slide fastener (zippered) storage pockets in doors; a swing-open windshield with an easy-acting center lever; a "natural grip" steering wheel, and more.

There were, early in 1932, "nine sparkling new models with gem-like body colors and upholstery in new pastel shades." Hardware fittings were in ebony with a silver finish. New lateral seat cushion springs lent added riding comfort, along with the adjustable shock absorbers.

The captions on the Essex advertisements were revealing: "It remakes the relation between luxury and cost!" "Listen now — quiet and solid as a rock." "The difference is its big car value!" "Why should you pay to be bumped around?" "There's a new power peak in the low-price field." "Things you don't see on the price ticket!" "News to the industry, but history to us!" And on and on.

Later in 1932 came the new, short-wheel-based Essex-Terraplane, which outwardly resembled the Essex except for its dual rows of hood louvres (one row above the others). In 1933, an Essex-Terraplane straight-eight was also available, this one with ventilating doors on each side of the hood.

During 1933, its name became, simply, Terraplane.

1933 Ford V-8

Though Fords were frequently advertised in color in magazines during 1931 (and throughout the 1928–1931 Model A era), for some strange reason Ford's use of U.S. magazine advertising nearly ceased during 1932 and 1933, not picking up again until 1934. One reason may have been that the all-new V-8 Ford for 1932 was not ready until the spring of 1932. However, Ford's higher-priced Lincoln cars were well advertised during 1932, and even in 1931. Fords were advertised in British magazines during that period.

In the thirties, Ford built Standard and De Luxe models; one could easily be distinguished from the other in 1938 through 1940, when each new Standard model bore a moderate (but not exact) resemblance to the previous year's De Luxe model. However, before 1938 there were other ways to tell the cars apart. In 1933, De Luxe models were identified by parking lamps on the cowl, two exterior horns instead of one, two taillights, and so on. Ford fans used to refer to these little luxuries as "dual equipment"; on the used-car lots, Fords with dual equipment were worth a few dollars more — and easy to sell.

1933 FORD

V8 SERIES "40"
with 221 C.I.D. L-HEAD
V-8 ENGINE (3 1/16" × 3 3/4")
75 H.P. @ 3800 RPM
5.5 TO 1 COMPRESSION
TOP SPEED = ABOUT 78 MPH
APPROX. 14 TO 18 M.P.G.
new 112" WHEELBASE
5.50 × 17 TIRES
4-WHEEL MECHANICAL BRAKES

DE LUXE MODELS = 2 HORNS,
2 TAIL-LIGHTS, SAFETY GLASS
ALL AROUND, ASH TRAY and
CIGAR LIGHTER.

DE LUXE TUDOR
(2-DOOR) SEDAN

STYLING OF 1934 IS
SIMILAR, BUT
1934 HAS TWO LATCH
HANDLES AT
EACH SIDE OF HOOD,
AND HEAVIER CHROME
BORDER AROUND GRILLE.

(4-CYL. MODELS STILL AVAIL.)

ORIGINAL F.O.B. (AT FACTORY)
PRICE: $ 550. 00
WEIGHT 2625 LBS.
4.33 GEAR RATIO

4-24-77

1934 De Soto Airflow

Anyone wanting a new De Soto in 1934 had to accept an ultra-streamlined Airflow — quite a change from De Soto's earlier models.

Chrysler Airflows were also produced (1934–1937), but in the Chrysler line there was also a conventionally styled model available, whereas during 1934, De Soto made all four of its body types as Airflows only. (In 1935, conservatively styled Airstream models were offered in both the Chrysler and De Soto lines, for there was considerable sales resistance to radically streamlined body types, especially to the racy fastback coupe seen in the background here.)

The Airflow cars offered many new features, including a "floating ride," with all passengers placed in the middle of the car. No longer was the back seat placed over the rear axle; now it rested *ahead* of it, thus making a great difference in riding comfort.

The color choices on the four 1934 De Soto Airflow bodies were bland: black, star blue, fisherman blue, explorer blue, Baden green, cedar bird, gunmetal, Palm Beach gray, Dorset gray, and a couple of sicklier choices — dusty gray and eel gray. Remember, 1934 was during the Depression, and these colors seemed ideal for avoiding creditors ("Just slip away, in a car of eel gray!"). In your new De Soto, you could almost blend in with the rocks by the side of the road and go unnoticed.

De Soto's Airflow series was discontinued after 1936. Not many buyers cared then, but in the years since, many Airflow enthusiasts have stepped forth to declare what truly advanced cars they were!

1935 Chrysler Airstream

The Chrysler Airstream for 1935 was offered to please those who wanted a newly styled Chrysler but not the extremely streamlined Airflow, which was considered too radical by many buyers.

The Airstream had the conservative styling of the Plymouths and Dodges, with a long, tapering hood. The chevron-styled grille was attractive (a similar grille was grafted onto the blunt nose of the Airflow in 1935). Airstream prices began at just $745 f.o.b., whereas Airflow prices were $1245–$5145 (a wide range, but then there were Airflows, Airflow Imperials, and Airflow Custom Imperials, with wheelbases up to 146 inches).

Like the Airflow, the Airstream offered Chrysler's famous "floating ride," because the rear seat and the engine had been moved forward to achieve a more scientific balance of weight; and the engine itself was suspended by "floating power," a spring-and-live-rubber mount system (which was first introduced on the Plymouth PA in June 1931 and virtually eliminated engine vibration). The front wheels had an independent spring system.

The foglights and spotlight on the convertible were optional.

1936 Auburn Speedster

"Style is what someone hopefully designs. It becomes a Fashion only when accepted by fashionable people" — according to an Auburn advertisement.

The renowned boat-tailed Auburn Speedster was introduced in the late twenties, but the model most fans know and admire is the long, narrow, superstreamlined 1935–1936 style (no speedster had been offered in 1934). The 1935 speedster was in Auburn's "851" series; the 1936 was "852."

By far the most famous of the boat-tailed (the rear resembling an overturned boat prow) speedsters, the Auburn was not the first. Even the low-priced Essex included a boat-tailed Speedabout roadster in its 1927 lineup. Other manufacturers building boat-tailed speedsters were Stutz, Franklin, and Packard. And there were such custom creations on Duesenberg and Rolls-Royce chassis.

Though $2245 was the advertised price of the Speedster, it's been reported that the total, delivered, out-the-door price was more than $3700 (including taxes, freight, etc.).

Each of the original 1935–1936 Speedsters was guaranteed to do at least 100 miles an hour, and they "loafed at 60," thanks to the centrifugal supercharger that added 35 horsepower (according to original reports).

What is the mystique of this timeless classic? An original Auburn ad explains: "When others honk raucously and race past, you are not disturbed if you sit behind the wheel of the new Super-Charged Auburn. You are content with the knowledge that you are driving the King of the Highway."

"Reissued" Auburn Speedsters, full-sized, close copies of the original models, are available today. Nobody is building straight-eight engines anymore, though, so these new Auburns are powered by V-8s.

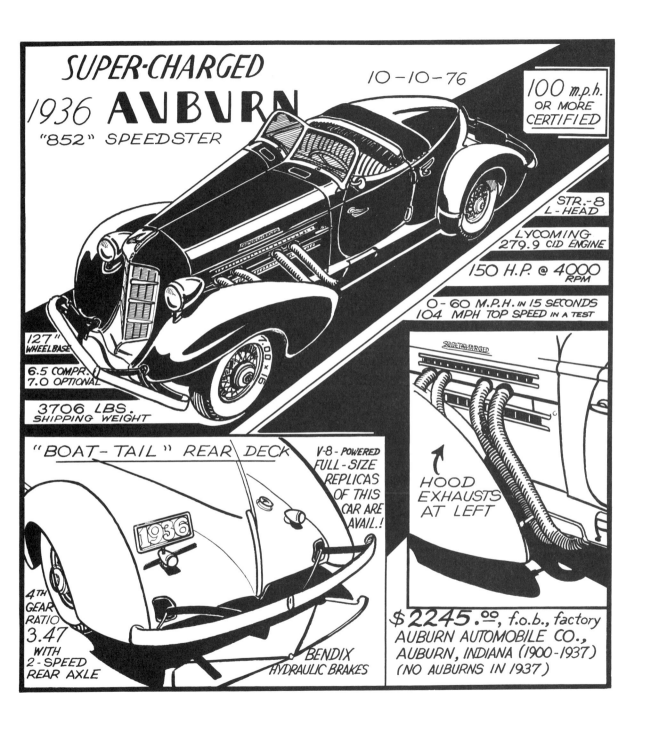

1937 Buick Century

Because of their classic beauty combined with rugged reliability, the Buicks of the later 1930s have been popular with collectors for many years. And the 1937 convertible is one of the best looking and most sought after of them all.

The styling was completely new for 1937, with a larger, more streamlined appearance. The 1937 and 1938 Buicks have much in common, though the 1937 has smaller, more closely spaced grille pieces. Some of the more expensive Buick sedans, such as the 90 Limited types, retained the old 1936 body profile.

The car's horsepower was increased, and 1937 Buick-Stromberg "Aerobat" carburetors were greatly improved, having two float bowls (placed before and behind the carburetor bar-

rels). This helped to prevent flooding or starving on grades, when going around sharp curves, and when decelerating suddenly.

It was amazing that the lowest-priced Buick Special 40 model could be sold for as little as $765 f.o.b. at the factory in Flint, Michigan, because it offered the beauty and class of the bigger models. Even the finest Buick Limiteds, like the Cadillacs in luxury, were priced below $2500.

The Century 60 was a well-liked series, as it was a medium-priced model but had the powerful engine of the big ones. A sedan in this series was tested at 86 miles an hour in high gear, but legend has it that the Buick Century was thus named because it would reach 100.

1937 Cord "812"

One of the most popular and eye-catching of all true classic cars was the 1937 Cord, with its squat, low-slung body following a long hood (accentuated by a unique wraparound horizontal grille). On supercharged models, there was the added excitement of chrome exhaust tubes protruding from the side of the hood.

Note the machine-turned metal dash of this Cord as well as the portrait of E. L. Cord, who had scored a fantastic success as the top salesman for Moon in the early 1920s and was wooed to the floundering Auburn Automobile Company in 1924 to put his shrewd selling talents to work there.

Cord was granted full control and a stock option. First, he had all the drab-looking Auburns in stock repainted in bright colors. The cars moved. And a straight-eight model became available.

And for 1925, Auburn was completely restyled, so it looked like no other car on the market. It was such a success that major restyling wasn't done again for six years.

Late in 1929, the company launched the new straight-eight L-29 Cord car, with front-wheel drive. A long-nosed classic, the big L-29 was continued to 1932; no further Cords were built until the smaller, streamlined 1936 "810" was introduced in late 1935. The "812" of 1937 was similar in appearance.

After the Cord was discontinued again, the 1936–1937 body dies were used by both Graham and Hupmobile (but with different hoods, grilles, and so on, and without front-wheel drive). And in the mid-sixties came new, shortened replicas of the 1936–1937 Cord convertibles.

I once saw and sketched a rare 1937 Cord three-window coupe (yellow with a black padded top). Only two of the coupes are said to exist. The coupe had a two-piece split rear window, as on the sedan.

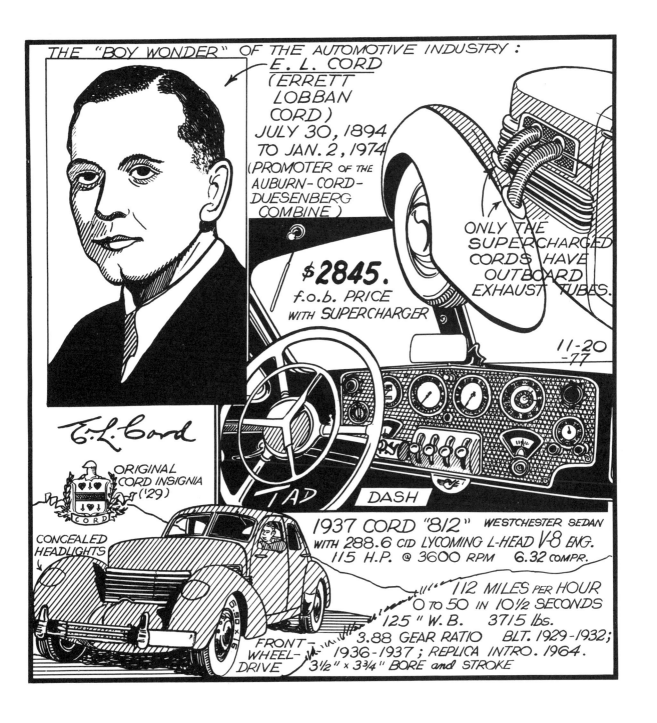

1937 Willys 4

There was quite a remarkable styling change in the 1937 Willys. The previous model (the "77") had been run for four seasons (1933–1936) with only minor styling changes. And though the "77" had looked good in 1933, it was undersized and dowdy and outdated for 1936.

The 1937 Willys still used an economical four-cyclinder L-head engine, but the all-steel body was streamlined and the car made considerably larger and wider than before. Its price made it less expensive than the popular Big Three (Chevrolet, Ford, and Plymouth), and buyers liked the marvelous fuel economy. Even during World War II, used Willys 4s were in great demand because of gas rationing.

With its economy of operation, the 1937 Willys was advertised to "pay for itself, by its savings, within 35,000 miles."

Six body colors, in Dulux synthetic baked enamel, were offered, and safety glass was used throughout.

Only two body types were available: the four-door sedan and the coupe, in standard or de luxe models.

1938 Duesenberg

Here's a most unusual Duesenberg! It differs in appearance from the typical Duesenberg, since it doesn't have the classic front-end styling of most 1929–1937 J and SJ models.

As Duesenberg bodies were custom-crafted by various coach builders to the orders of each buyer, a few of those who bought the later models saw fit to "modernize" the styling; some classic car buffs consider such variants "desecrations," distinctive as they may be.

The body for this particular Duesenberg was originally chosen to be built by Erdmann and Rossi in Germany. But the job was, instead, awarded to Rollston (New York); the bill for the body alone came to $9043.

The top speed of an SJ (supercharged) Duesenberg was said to be 130 miles an hour, but when this particular specimen was road-tested in 1959 for a magazine report, the age of the vehicle — and the weight of its massive town car body — held it back.

The first car after this to bear the Duesenberg name was the 1966 model that was sold to the Wrigley family (famed chewing gum manufacturers). Eventually, though, there was another "Duesie" revival, as in recent years there have also been new Cords and Auburns, and even a revival of the Stutz.

1938 Ford Standard V-8 "60"

Unless you've long been a fan of early Ford V-8s or personally recall when the cars of the 1930s were new, you might not have known that from 1937 to 1940, Ford offered an alternate, *smaller* V-8 engine of 60 horsepower, with only 136-cubic-inch displacement (compared to the full-sized 221 c.i.d. engine). The 60-horsepower model gave wonderful fuel economy but was not popular. Most people who bought Ford V-8s liked the power, speed, and flashing acceleration of the 85-horsepower model and could not get used to the little "60." Consequently, used "60s" had far less resale value on the car lots.

Speaking of used Fords, one Ford advertisement of 1938 claimed that there were still more than one million Model Ts (1909 to 1927 models) still in service, still licensed! And many years later, in the 1960s, there were still one million of Ford's 1928 to 1931 Model As on the road! In fact, Model Ts and As are more commonly found today than the Ford "60s," even though the latter were built more recently.

The 1938 Ford "60" was lighter, but no smaller, than the 85-horsepower version. The Standard models of 1938 to 1940 generally looked a year older than their De Luxe counterparts. The 1938 Standard, for example, somewhat resembled the 1937 Ford, except the grille and hood louvres were joined as one unit, unlike the 1937.

In 1938, visitors were invited to see Ford's mammoth Rouge Plant in Dearborn, Michigan; during the preceding year, nearly a million people from all over the world had toured portions of Ford's 1096-acre main factory. In those days, one might even have had a glimpse of old Henry Ford himself, for he took an active part in the management of things until 1945, when his grandson Henry Ford II was granted control.

1938 Studebaker

Notice the streamlined, sunken headlights and separate parking lights on this 1938 Studebaker State President. The low-priced Studebakers that year had conventional, bullet-shaped headlights mounted atop the fenders, and parking lights were separate.

Studebaker's advertising in 1938 urged prospective customers to take just a ten-minute demonstration ride in one of the new models: "See how much better it runs, rides, steers, brakes, accelerates, climbs hills and handles by comparison with any other car you've tried."

Studebakers were built in South Bend, Indiana, by "7,300 master craftsmen." The company had been established in 1852, first making wheelbarrows and horse-drawn rigs. Studebaker electric cars appeared in 1902, joined by gas-powered models in 1904.

The final Studebakers were built at the Canadian branch factory in 1966, but since that time the Avanti II sports model has been produced in South Bend by a small, dedicated organization composed of many former Studebaker employees.

Other features offered on this 1938 model included independent planar front-wheel suspension, a built-in Fram oil economizer, a hypoid gear rear axle, a one-piece steel body of "battleship construction," a 55-inch-wide front seat for three, and, of course, hydraulic brakes and safety glass.

Studebaker did not merge with Packard until the 1950s, yet there is a "Packard-ish" look to the stylish rear section of this distinctive club sedan.

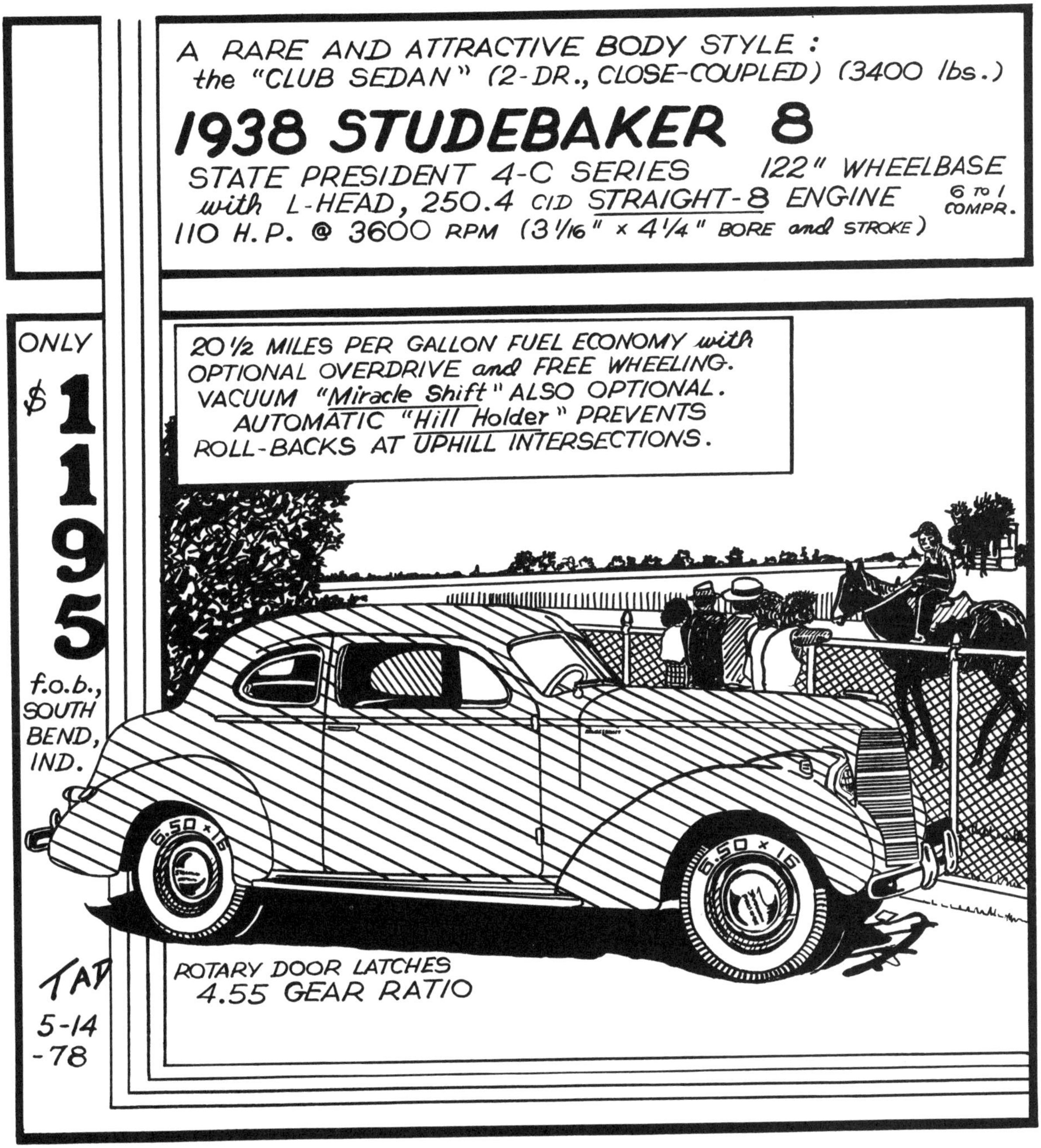

A RARE AND ATTRACTIVE BODY STYLE :
the "CLUB SEDAN" (2-DR., CLOSE-COUPLED) (3400 lbs.)

1938 STUDEBAKER 8

STATE PRESIDENT 4-C SERIES   122" WHEELBASE
with L-HEAD, 250.4 CID STRAIGHT-8 ENGINE   6 TO 1 COMPR.
110 H.P. @ 3600 RPM (3 1/16" × 4 1/4" BORE and STROKE)

ONLY
$
1195
f.o.b.,
SOUTH
BEND,
IND.

20 1/2 MILES PER GALLON FUEL ECONOMY with OPTIONAL OVERDRIVE and FREE WHEELING. VACUUM "Miracle Shift" ALSO OPTIONAL. AUTOMATIC "Hill Holder" PREVENTS ROLL-BACKS AT UPHILL INTERSECTIONS.

ROTARY DOOR LATCHES
4.55 GEAR RATIO

TAD
5-14
-78

American automobile construction was suspended from February 1942 to July 1945 so that all effort could be focused on vital military production. Used cars were at a premium during the war, and even some forgotten relics from the 1920s and early thirties were dusted off and pressed into commuter service, transporting workers to factories and shipyards.

This 1942 Chevrolet Blackout model is an example of the very last cars built before production shut down. New trucks were still available during most of the war, but only by special priority to qualified workers or professionals in essential jobs.

After the war, Henry J. Kaiser teamed with Joe Frazer to create the new Kaiser and Frazer cars. Crosley reemerged as a more serious small contender than it had been before the war. During the 1940s, the independent companies (including Hudson, Nash, Studebaker, Packard, and Willys) were still holding their own in the market. After the war, the seller could name his own price for a time, because there were not enough new cars to meet the demand. Waiting lists for new cars were the rule in 1946, and some buyers got on several waiting lists simultaneously, reselling their new cars for big profits each time because buyers with money were often willing to pay much more than list price for a new car in order to get one quickly.

War clouds were gathering as the 1940s began. Another conflict was under way in Europe, and America was drawn into the battle on December 7, 1941, when Japan attacked the U.S. naval fleet at Pearl Harbor. President Roosevelt died in April 1945 and was succeeded by his Vice-President, Harry S Truman. Truman proved himself a popular leader and was reelected in 1948.

The postwar boom was slowed temporarily by the business recession of 1948–1949, which hurt most of the smaller independent auto manufacturers.

Radio was still the king of home entertainment, but *after* the 1940s, the top comedy and drama shows would move to television.

The popular songs of the 1940s were heard on radio's "Hit Parade" each week and included: "When You Wish upon a Star" (1940), "Intermezzo" (1941), "Jingle, Jangle, Jingle" (1942), "Praise the Lord and Pass the Ammunition" (1942), "There's a Star-Spangled Banner Waving Somewhere" (1942), "Comin' In on a Wing and a Prayer" (1943), "I'll Be Seeing You" (1944), "Sentimental Journey" (1944), "It's Been a Long, Long Time" (1945), "Rum and Coca-Cola" (1945), "Anniversary Song" (1946), "To Each His Own" (1946), "I Wonder, I Wonder, I Wonder" (1947), "Buttons and Bows" (1948), and "Some Enchanted Evening" (1949).

The Action Era

The 1940s

1940 De Soto

The 1940 De Soto S-7 series claimed thirty-nine important new features "not found in any '36, '37, or '38 car." Among the new developments: an all-new body with larger windows; a longer wheelbase; the new "floating ride," with the rear axle moved back 7½ inches and passengers cradled between the axles; sealed-beam headlights; wider seats; warning lights on dash gauges (to call the driver's attention to deficiencies); a full lower edge on rear side doors (as they now cleared the rear fenders); new door insulation; a larger trunk, with the spare tire placed against the right side; a gravel shield between the rear bumper and the body; an optional new heating and ventilating system; an improved version of the steering column gearshift — and more. In spite of the many luxuries, De Soto prices were set $20 to $48 *lower* than they had been in 1939.

A convertible coupe was available in the Custom series, and it had a power-operated top. Runningboards were optional, and overdrive was available.

As in previous years, Major Bowes advertised the new De Soto on his CBS radio amateur hour each Thursday evening between 9:00 and 10:00 P.M., Eastern Standard Time.

1941 Divco-Twin

"Oh, I remember seeing those around for years! Yes, I used to see them around town everywhere, but I never knew what kind of truck they were." This is a typical reaction to the Divco-Twin (or just plain Divco) stand-up delivery truck.

Because of their operating economy and the large amount of headroom inside, these Divco trucks would be ideal, today, for conversion to small motor homes. By adding a couple of windows, paneling the inside walls, and installing sleeping, kitchen, and bath facilities, a truck of this type would become a small motor home of surprising economy and simplicity. The only problem is that there aren't many of these little trucks available any longer.

Nevertheless, for more than three decades,
the Divco was a common sight on city and suburban streets, everywhere that milk was delivered from house to house. Remember how those glass bottles rattled around in the cage-like metal carrying case when the milkman brought them to your door? (There was even a song, in the early 1940s, called "Milkman, Keep Those Bottles Quiet!")

Divco was an independent company until the mid-1930s; then for a few years it was affiliated with Twin Coach — thus the Divco-Twin name until after World War II, when once again it became Divco. Later it was known as Divco-Wayne, following another consolidation.

The trucks, now using six-cylinder Ford engines, are still available on special order from the Divco Truck Company in Delaware, Ohio.

1941 Nash Ambassador 600

This little beauty may evoke pleasant memories for many people. For 1941, Nash introduced an economy model that was packed with new features.

Truly, the "600" was economical. American Motors Corporation, which developed from the 1954 merger of Nash and Hudson, states that the "600" designation meant that, under favorable conditions and with overdrive, the new model would travel as far as six hundred miles on one tank of fuel.

Although some people used to refer to the old Nashes as "gutless wonders" (since their acceleration sometimes left much to be desired), the Nash engines were quiet, reliable, and outstandingly easy on gas. The L-head Nash engine was unusually plain and simple-looking, since the manifold (which is bolted on in most other engines) was mysteriously concealed. On this particular engine, it was simply built into the block itself.

Another unusual Nash feature, dating back to 1936, was the optional seatbed; this was handy for overnight family camping trips. Nash was not the first car with this feature, but Nash is better remembered for it than such cars as the 1919 Pan and the 1931 Durant, which also featured seatbeds.

The unitized body-and-frame is common-place nowadays, but it made the 1941 Nash different — a very solid difference, making it free from most squeaks and rattles.

Some reviewers of 1941 considered the Nash "600" to be the outstanding car of the year. And during the gas rationing, the commuting, and the car pools of World War II, the Nash "600" came through a winner. When it came to full-sized cars, only the four-cylinder Willys was as inexpensive to drive.

1942 Chevrolet

For 1942, Chevrolet offered three series: Master Deluxe, Special Deluxe, and Fleetline (the first two series eventually became the Stylemaster and Fleetmaster).

There were numerous minor changes in addition to the new "fade-away" front fender treatment. The so-called American Eagle grille was new, and it incorporated the parking lights at each edge. The hood was longer and larger.

The dash had only minor decoration changes. The interior trim and upholstery patterns were new: Fleetline models had brown upholstery, the others had gray.

The 1942 model was advertised as "the finest Chevrolet of all time." This claim might annoy fans of the 1941 Chevrolet, the 1957, the 1932, and many other vintage Chevrolet models that have fiercely loyal followings.

Because it was in production only a short time, the 1942 is scarce in comparison to other Chevrolets. It wasn't even a common sight in the 1940s. During World War II, anyone owning a 1942 car was looked on with envy or awe, for most of the 1942 cars had been carefully rationed out to buyers with wartime priorities, jobs essential to the war effort.

And the Blackout models, which had no chrome, were scarcest of all. They were not especially liked when new because most customers preferred plenty of chrome and thought that any car without it looked "cheap."

In time, this once-scorned Blackout model has become extremely desirable because of its historical significance and its scarcity.

1942 CHEVROLET
116" WHEELBASE
6 CYL. I-HEAD ENGINE
3½" × 3¾" BORE + STR.
216½ CU. IN. DISPL.
90 HP @ 3300 RPM
PRICED FROM
$799.,
f.o.b.

4.11 GEAR RATIO

DASH

A RARE "BLACKOUT COUPE!"

5-13-79

BECAUSE OF WORLD WAR II, CIVILIAN CAR PRODUCTION WAS SUSPENDED FROM FEB., 1942 TO JULY, 1945. 258,795 1942 CHEVROLETS WERE BUILT. THE FINAL '42s WERE "BLACKOUT" MODELS, WITH PAINTED TRIM INSTEAD OF CHROME. A FEW EVEN ADAPTED WOODEN BUMPERS TO SPARE THE STEEL FOR THE WAR EFFORT.

LESS THAN 2350 SUCH "BLACKOUT" COUPES BUILT BY CHEV. IN EARLY '42.

TAD

DETAILS THANKS TO E. R. GILLESPIE, LINCOLN, NEB.

new 1942 "FADEAWAY" FENDERS BLEND INTO DOORS.
6.00 × 16 TIRES

1943 Dodge War Wagon

If you like old "woodies," this car should truly interest you, as it may well be the rarest of all wooden-bodied cars from the 1940s.

Though American civilian automobile production was suspended from February 1942 until July 1945, this Dodge War Wagon was a 1943 model, since it was revealed in the December 1942 issue of *Motor* magazine.

The Brooklyn, New York, Dodge agency of Bishop, McCormick & Bishop sought to create a multipurpose wartime vehicle by making the "Three-in-One War Wagon." With "the assistance of Dodge engineers and the Derham Custom Body Co.," a Dodge four-door sedan was altered by the addition of an expanded rear wooden body extension. This made the vehicle resemble the old-time depot hacks, which preceded the modern station wagon, as additional passengers were seated sideways in the open-sided rear quarters. A rolled canopy could be lowered in bad weather.

The War Wagon was created to serve as a fifteen-passenger car pool bus, a four-stretcher ambulance, or a one-ton truck. The rear springs were strengthened to carry the added weight (its body weighed 540 pounds more than the standard sedan). A Dodge truck (dual-wheel) rear axle was fitted. The floor of the wooden body extension was at the level of the sedan's rear seat cushion.

Bishop, McCormick & Bishop hoped to produce more of these unusual "woodies," but only the pilot model is remembered. The War Wagon was sanctioned by the Office of Price Administration, and it was driven around Brooklyn and the vicinity while approval for more units was sought from the War Production Board.

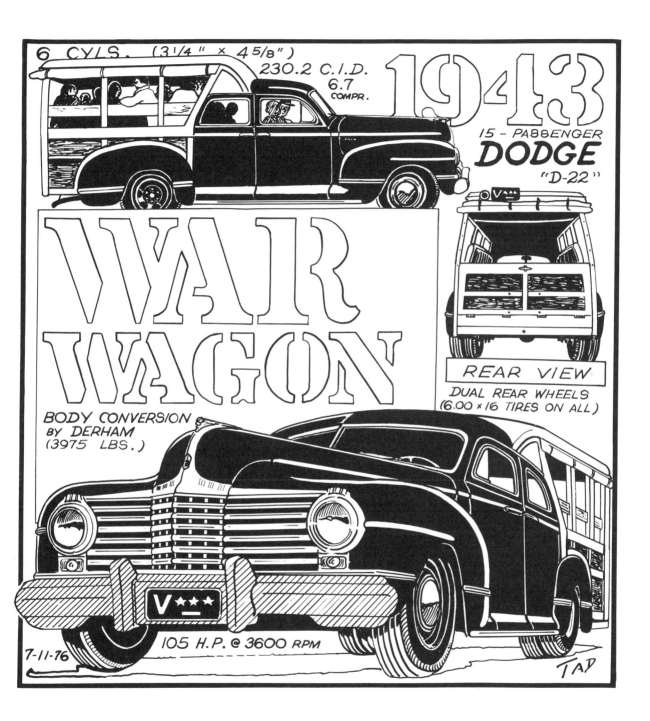

6 CYLS. (3 1/4" × 4 5/8") 230.2 C.I.D. 6.7 COMPR.

1943

15 - PASSENGER
DODGE
"D-22"

WAR WAGON

BODY CONVERSION
BY DERHAM
(3975 LBS.)

REAR VIEW
DUAL REAR WHEELS
(6.00 × 16 TIRES ON ALL)

V ★★★

7-11-76

105 H.P. @ 3600 RPM

TAD

1945 Ford Truck

Most of Ford's conventional trucks from 1942 to 1947 resembled this 1945 model. (Before 1942, Ford's truck grille somewhat resembled that of the 1939 Ford de luxe cars.)

Trucks were more readily available to civilian buyers with "priorities" during World War II — except in 1943 and early 1944, when new truck production was basically for the military.

Notice the Spartan appearance of the cab in this truck. Today's truck cabs are comfortable, even luxurious. The older ones, though, could be dangerous to occupants in case of sudden stops or minor collisions, for door interiors and other sections were often lined with steel or fiberboard, and they had no seat belts or padded dashboards.

But there are still a good number of old trucks in regular service. And because of their stark simplicity, the interiors of old trucks can be easily restored by collectors today.

1945 Gordon Diamond

"What is it?" That was a commonly asked question around San Francisco Bay in the late 1940s and 1950s any time the odd Gordon Diamond was seen on the street. The car had much in common with Buckminster Fuller's famous Dymaxion. Both had streamlined bodies built over tubular steel cages, with Ford V-8 engines mounted near the rear, and both had side access doors. However, the Dymaxion of the 1930s had a balsa outer skin, while the Gordon Diamond was all steel.

In a telephone conversation a few years ago, H. Gordon Hansen informed me that he had been living in San Lorenzo, California (near Oakland), when he had conceived and built the car. Later, he moved across the bay to Sunnyvale, near San Jose.

Built as a personal idea car and as an experiment, the Gordon Diamond was the object of a $17,000 promotional expenditure by its builder, who hoped to sell the concept to a major automobile manufacturer. Both Kaiser-Frazer and Packard showed some interest, and Bank of America was briefly interested in financing Hansen's project so that more Diamonds could be produced. But these deals ultimately failed to go through. The car was so different that investors were scared of it.

Hansen put ninety-five thousand miles on this car, and in 1967 he sold it to Harrah's Automobile Collection in Reno, Nevada.

Since both the front and rear wheels steer, the turning radius is only 12 feet. Steering is easy, too, as half the car's weight rests on the central (powered) wheels. With the wide, diamond-shaped wheel distribution, the car glides easily over ruts and chuckholes, with no dipping or jouncing over rough spots.

1945 GORDON DIAMOND

BLT. AT SAN LORENZO, CALIFORNIA, BY
H. GORDON HANSEN

UNIQUE "DIAMOND" WHEEL PLAN with STEERABLE
SINGLE FRONT and REAR WHEEL (156" WHEELBASE
BETWEEN FR. and REAR HUBS.) 2 WHEELS ALSO
PLACED "AMIDSHIP" FOR TRACTION and STABILITY. THIS
ONE-OF-A-KIND VEHICLE SOLD by MR. HANSEN in 1967,
TO HARRAH'S AUTOMOBILE COLLECTION, RENO, NEVADA.

STEEL BODY with TUBULAR STEEL FRAMEWORK
62" HIGH   (TOP SPEED = 95)   WT. = 3750 lbs.
80" WIDE

DESIGNED 1943, BLT. 1945, COMPLETED AND LICENSED 1947.

FORD V-8 TRUCK ENGINE (L-HEAD, 100 H.P.) AHEAD of REAR WHEEL.

TAD

9-20-81

1946 Mercury

Until the mid-1948 introduction of the all-new 1949 model, which was a much larger and heavier-looking car than its predecessors, the Mercury was very similar to its slightly lower-priced brother the Ford, except for a different grille, different dash and trim, a slight difference in engine size and horsepower, and so on.

The Ford Motor Company had first introduced its Mercury V-8 for 1939, creating a car to fill the price and size gap between the Ford V-8 and the Lincoln V-12. The Mercury was closer to the Ford than to the Lincoln in all aspects until the big 1949 models came along.

As World War II came to a close in the summer of 1945, the new Fords and Mercurys appeared, the long-awaited 1946 models. "Step Out with Mercury" was Mercury's first postwar slogan. But this was shortly replaced by a new 1946 slogan: "More of Everything You Want with Mercury." Meaning, of course, that Ford fans would get more of all the Ford features and qualities they liked if they spent just a few dollars more and purchased a Mercury.

This new Mercury was advertised, in color, in many popular magazines. And it was advertised on radio on the Ford–Bob Crosby show on CBS. (Telecasting was very limited in 1946 and was seen only on a few thousand sets in the greater New York City area.)

Mercury's features for 1946 included a new grille, an improved instrument panel, a choice of two-tone fabric interiors, and nineteen engine improvements, such as tri-alloy bearings, a new oil pump, new balanced carburetion, and four-ring aluminum pistons for greater gas and oil economy.

1947 Kaiser

"Find a need, and fill it," Henry J. Kaiser often said. A western industrialist who made a fortune in steel, cement, and shipbuilding enterprises, Kaiser decided, in the mid-1940s, to join forces with an experienced automobile producer, Joseph W. Frazer, and manufacture cars after World War II.

By that time, it was almost impossible for a new automobile manufacturer to compete with the established giants. But Kaiser had an available supply of precious steel as well as the foundation of the old Graham-Paige Company to build on. And there was a drastic postwar shortage of new cars. In the period from 1946 to 1948, most auto dealers put their customers on long waiting lists. When they finally got their cars, some customers immediately resold them at large profits to other buyers who had more money than patience.

So the small "independent" automakers were able to hold their own because of the unsatisfied demand for more and more new cars. By mid-'47, over one hundred thousand Kaiser and Frazer cars had been sold in spite of the public's usual apprehension about "unproven" names. Reliable Continental six-cylinder L-head engines were used in Kaiser-Frazer products.

Eclipsed in 1950 by Kaiser's compact Henry J, the Frazer was discontinued during the 1951 model year. The 1951 Kaiser was a beautiful thing, but in 1955 Kaiser's manufacturing operations were transferred to Argentina. There, the Kaiser Carabela was built until 1962.

1949 Crosley

Standing 6 feet 4 inches tall, Powel Crosley, Jr., was a big man, both in physical and business stature. And he was a man of integrity who was successful in many fields. During the 1920s he was a pioneer in the mass production of inexpensive radios, enabling many more people to enjoy this new luxury in their homes. He also owned radio stations (including WLW in Cincinnati) as well as the Cincinnati Reds baseball team and even their home stadium, Crosley Field. He also built refrigerators, TV sets, washing machines, and other appliances (including a novel electrical device to restore balding hairlines).

Though a millionaire, Crosley did not lust after money but gained pleasure in giving his customers an honest value. He frequently cut the prices of his products after devising more economical methods of production, thereby sharing the savings with customers.

The early Crosley cars (1939–1942) were diminutive two-cylinder putt-putts, cute to look at but somewhat toylike. Some were sold at Macy's department store (though *not* in the toy department). After World War II, Crosley reentered the automotive market with four-cylinder models. A man named Taylor designed a new engine, which had been used in military generators during the war, and Crosley bought the design. The Taylor engine was unique in that it was entirely stamped, not cast, and the hundred and twenty stamped components and tubing were copper-brazed together. For this reason, it was named the CO-BRA engine.

The stamped engine turned 5400 rpm at only 40 miles an hour and topped out at 10,000 rpm, like a tiny hummingbird. With this high metabolism, it tended to wear out after 25,000 miles, so for 1949, a cast-iron engine of similar dimensions (44 c.i.d.) was substituted. Soon Crosley offered these improved CIBA engines at a ridiculously low price to all those owning an older Crosley who wished to trade in their worn-out "tin" engines. It was a generous gesture on Crosley's part, almost like fulfilling a guarantee that had never been offered!

During 1949 Crosley also developed the peppy Hotshot Super Sport roadster.

By 1949, over sixty thousand Crosleys had been sold. However, gas was cheap in those days, about 23 cents a gallon, and most motorists wanted their cars bigger and more powerful each time they bought a new one. Few people preferred to ride in dinky vehicles just to get 35 to 50 miles per gallon. After suffering a three-year sales decline and having to dig into his own pockets repeatedly to keep the little company going, Powel Crosley decided to throw in the towel and sell out in 1952. The car factory was sold to General Tire Company.

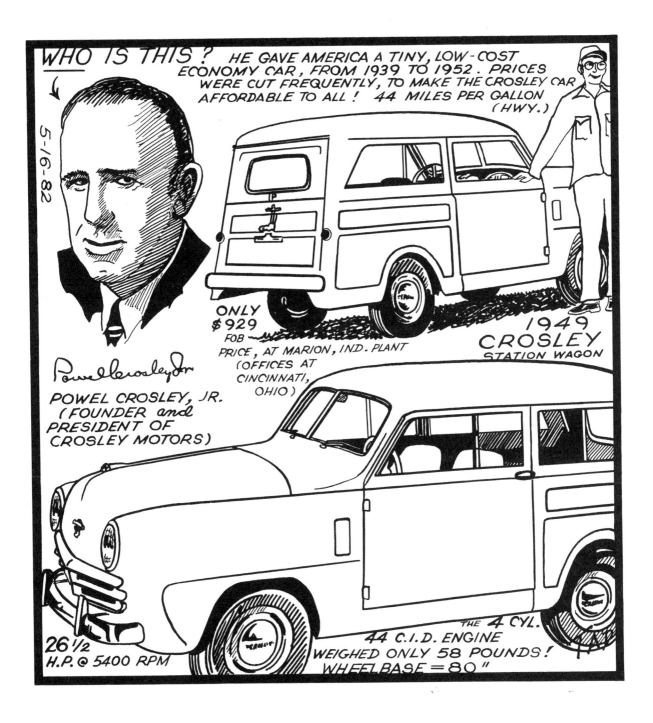

WHO IS THIS?

HE GAVE AMERICA A TINY, LOW-COST ECONOMY CAR, FROM 1939 TO 1952. PRICES WERE CUT FREQUENTLY, TO MAKE THE CROSLEY CAR AFFORDABLE TO ALL! 44 MILES PER GALLON (HWY.)

5-16-82

ONLY $929 FOB PRICE, AT MARION, IND. PLANT (OFFICES AT CINCINNATI, OHIO)

1949 CROSLEY STATION WAGON

Powel Crosley Jr

POWEL CROSLEY, JR. (FOUNDER and PRESIDENT OF CROSLEY MOTORS)

26 1/2 H.P. @ 5400 RPM

THE 4 CYL. 44 C.I.D. ENGINE WEIGHED ONLY 58 POUNDS! WHEELBASE = 80"

1949 Plymouth Suburban

The Chrysler Corporation was a few weeks late in getting its all-new 1949 models on the market (in February), and so, for a time, held-over 1948 models were tagged "early 1949."

This car, though, is a true 1949 (second series) model, one of the totally restyled types. Also new in 1949 was this all-metal two-door Suburban wagon, offered on the shorter-wheelbase (111 inches) P-17 chassis. Like the four-door "woodies," the metal Suburban had a two-piece window in the upper tailgate.

Starting in 1949, Chrysler cars (which included De Soto, Dodge, and Chrysler) adopted a trim new "boxy" look: smaller but wider, with flatter sides and front fenders that blended with the body.

The "Plymouth Builds Great Cars" slogan was continued along with a new one: "The Car That Likes to Be Compared."

From the late 1930s, Plymouth dealers and advertisements frequently displayed comparison charts, sizing up Plymouth features against those of competitors.

In 1949, for example, Plymouth claimed twenty-one of the twenty-two "costly features" found in high-priced cars, while "low-priced car No. 2" had only thirteen of these features and "low-priced car No. 3" had but four of them. The horsepower was slightly increased with the new 7:1 compression ratio. The instrument panels were redesigned, with three circular instrument groups at left (the speedometer was in the middle circle). An electric automatic choke was added, and new circuit-breakers made fuses unnecessary.

The 1949 Plymouth consisted of "13,000 parts," many of them all new. Little remained of the 1946–1948 P-15 look, though the P-15 had been in production over three years and had become a nearly perfect car.

Business slowed down in the early fifties but picked up again with vigor in 1955, which became one of Detroit's most golden years. And one of the prettiest cars was the totally restyled 1951 Kaiser.

The 1950s became the era of the "horsepower race," as various makes of cars began to switch to hot, overhead-valve V-8 engines and offer all kinds of electrical and power-operated gadgets.

The 1950s brought the last models of the Crosley, Kaiser, Frazer, Nash, Hudson, and Packard. And with 1954 came the last of the old straight-eight engines (in Packard and Pontiac). The V-8 engine reigned supreme by the end of the decade, which also saw the climax of the "big tailfin" era, exemplified by the 1959 Cadillac. Chrome trim was also popular throughout the 1950s.

Volkswagen "Beetles" and other small imported cars were cutting into Detroit's business, however, and American producers gradually countered the trend by developing their own compact cars. But the Volkswagen invasion was light compared to the heavy onslaught of Japanese imports that gathered momentum in the 1960s and 1970s and caused added trouble for Detroit.

From today's perspective, the 1950s seem like a prosperous period. But at the time, many considered it an age of uncertainty, even an age of anxiety, as the West felt threatened by communism and the Cold War. From 1950 to 1953, the United States was deeply involved in the Korean War. In 1952, the Republican and former general Dwight D. "Ike" Eisenhower was elected President. After the Korean War, there was an era of relative calm. Ike was reelected in 1956, and peace continued, though marred by a recession in 1957–1958.

By the end of the fifties, nearly every U.S. household had at least one television set, and most of the shows formerly on radio could now be seen as well as heard. Radio continued as a popular medium for top-forty DJ shows and talk shows as well as for newscasting.

Popular music drifted from banal sweetness to guitar-thumping rock and new-sound novelty in the course of the decade. The first strange new voice of the 1950s belonged to Johnny Ray, who in 1952 made a pair of hits on one record: "Cry" and "The Little White Cloud That Cried." Partially deaf, Ray had a dissonant voice that titillated those seeking something new.

But in 1956, Elvis Presley eclipsed all his rivals with the help of clever promotion by his manager, Colonel Tom Parker, and by appearing on the right TV shows at the right times. Presley, whose early gimmick was wild gyrations onstage, had his imitators, but he was soon proclaimed "the King of Rock-'n'-Roll." Elvis made several movies as well as millions of records, and many of his loyal fans made the pilgrimage to the gates of his mansion in Nashville, "Graceland."

Some of the songs of the fifties are: "If I Knew You Were Comin' I'd Have Baked a Cake" (1950), "My Heart Cries for You" (1951), "Tennessee Waltz" (1951), "Wheel of Fortune" (1952), "Vaya con Dios" (1953), "Rock Around the Clock" (1954), "Three Coins in the Fountain" (1954), "Heart" (1955), "Autumn Leaves" (1956), "Hound Dog" (1956), "True Love" (1956), "Tammy" (1957), "He's Got the Whole World in His Hands" (1958), and "El Paso" (1959).

The Cold War
and a
Time of Expansion

The 1950s

1950 Hudson Pacemaker 500

Dyed-in-the-wool "Hudsonites" know that 1948 was the first great year for Hudson's all-new postwar styling and that the 1950 models were the first to include the new, inverted V bars on the grille. This grille was introduced on the lower-priced Pacemaker, a new series for 1950 through 1952.

Motor Trend magazine (which began publication in September 1949) road-tested a 1950 Pacemaker and wrote it up in its February 1950 issue. The transmission in the test car was manual, but the Hudson cork clutch and helical-cut gears made it easy to "speed shift" and made gear-clashing almost impossible (except when accidentally shifting to reverse when moving forward in low).

The 18.2:1 steering-gear ratio made the new Pacemaker easy to park and gave a feeling at the wheel of always having "positive control." The new model cornered well, without the excessive leanover or tire squeal so typical of other cars in that era.

The car could be lugged down to 8 miles an hour in high without bucking (though many fine cars of the 1920s could lug down to 3 in high!).

In acceleration tests, the new Pacemaker did 0–60 miles an hour through the gears in 16.45 seconds in overdrive (and in 15.38 seconds not using overdrive). In quarter-mile speed runs, the average was 87.73 miles an hour.

For 1953, the Pacemaker was replaced by Hudson's smaller, compact Jet.

1950 Oldsmobile "88"

Should one interview a large number of Oldsmobile fans to determine the most popular model among collectors, the resounding majority would surely vote for the 1950 Olds, especially the peppy "88," with its hot-performing overhead-valve V-8 engine, which had been introduced the previous year. Convertibles and two-door hardtops are especially favored.

The 1950 "88" was a remarkable performer in comparison to most other cars of its day. Remember, it was an era in which flathead sixes and long straight-eights were still dominant.

In 1950, Olds captured the limelight in the NASCAR Grand National racing circuit, winning first place in the famous Mexican Road Race. The 1950 was the last of the swift, light, sporty-looking Oldsmobiles for some time to come. The 1951 was enlarged and had mushier suspension and is not as widely admired by collectors.

In addition to the "88," there were also the six-cylinder "76" series of 1950 and the larger "98" V-8. The "98" was bulkier (by today's standards less attractive), and it was a hint of what the 1951s would be like.

Hydra-Matic automatic transmission was a popular option, but most of today's "88" admirers prefer those with a manual shift, for they're considerably more nimble in acceleration.

1951 Kaiser

This car may look strange today, but in early 1950 (when the 1951 Kaiser-Frazer models appeared long before their competitors') it was sensational.

The Frazer, about to be discontinued, was not as dramatically designed as the Kaiser, save for a most unusual grille, new taillights, and the like. But this 1951 Kaiser looked entirely new from one end to the other. The car looked big, yet it still seemed light and nimble because of its large expanses of glass.

Kaiser-Frazer cars were the last noncommercial vehicles to use Continental engines in quantity, though many truck manufacturers continued to use ready-made engines such as Continental, Hercules, Buda, Cummins, or Detroit diesels to hold down production costs.

It's easy to spot a 1951 Kaiser. It's the only one with this body style to use a two-piece V windshield. The final 1954–1955 Kaisers used a similar body, but with many styling modifications (a new grille, taillights, etc.). (After 1955, the Kaiser was continued in Argentina for nearly seven more years as the Carabela.)

Kaiser-Frazer fans are very loyal, and there is an excellent worldwide club for owners and admirers of these interesting cars.

1953 Ford

The Ford Motor Company observed its Golden Anniversary year with a 1953 model acclaimed in advertising as "The New Standard of the American Road" with "41 Worth More Features."

Because all the 1952 Ford cars had been totally restyled, the 1953 changes were less obvious. The grille featured one modified "spinner" (instead of three, as on the 1952 and 1954 models).

As in 1952, there were three types of station wagons: the two-door, all-metal ranch wagon; the four-door, all-metal country sedan; and the de luxe, four-door Country Squire, decorated with two-tone wood and wood-grain side trim.

Ford side doors now included two-position checks: they could be held either half-way or fully opened. This was an improvement over 1952, when some riders squawked that Ford's quick-closing doors would paddle their fannies before they could scramble inside.

A countersprung trunk lid required little effort to raise. Likewise, steering required little effort, and manual steering was almost as easy as the power steering found on some expensive new cars.

However, one auto-test writer complained that the car had a tendency to wander unless continually set straight, and he suggested the installation of the tighter F-1 Ford truck steering gear.

Both L-head V-8 and Mileage Maker OHV six engines were available. The Strato-Star V-8 was sluggish at a crawl, but peppy on pickup at speeds over 30 miles an hour.

As it had for many years, Ford offered special Ford batteries and Ford spark plugs. Female Ford fans could even buy Motor Mate fashion coats, especially designed to harmonize with the 1953 Ford colors and decor.

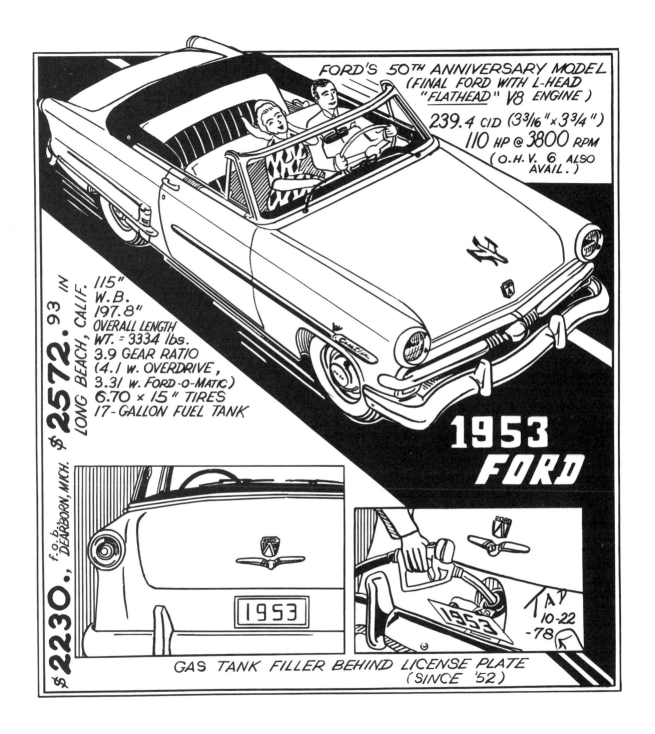

FORD'S 50TH ANNIVERSARY MODEL
(FINAL FORD WITH L-HEAD
"FLATHEAD" V8 ENGINE)
239.4 CID (3³/₁₆" × 3³/₄ ")
110 HP @ 3800 RPM
(O.H.V. 6 ALSO
AVAIL.)

115"
W.B.
197.8"
OVERALL LENGTH
WT. = 3334 lbs.
3.9 GEAR RATIO
(4.1 w. OVERDRIVE,
3.31 w. FORD-O-MATIC)
6.70 × 15" TIRES
17-GALLON FUEL TANK

$2572.93 IN LONG BEACH, CALIF.

$2230., f.o.b. DEARBORN, MICH.

1953 FORD

1953

1953

TAD
10-22
-78

GAS TANK FILLER BEHIND LICENSE PLATE
(SINCE '52)

1953 Mercedes-Benz Diesel

Mercedes-Benz of North America issued a press release in 1976 stating that this 1953 diesel-powered model of its "170" series was aiming for an all-time endurance record, having covered over 789,000 miles and still going strong! Its owner, in Pennsylvania, hoped that it would last a million miles or more.

The original engine was used for over 625,000 miles. Then, when it failed to maintain its former oil pressure level, a used 1951 engine was substituted.

In its press release, Mercedes-Benz added that it had been driven the equivalent of more than *thirty-one times the distance around the earth!*

The owner of the car was a retired tool and die maker who previously commuted 138 miles a day to and from his job and traveled from 700 to 1600 miles per week. He had purchased the car, used, in 1958, when it had only 60,000-plus miles on its odometer. Earlier he had owned another Mercedes-Benz, a diesel model 180-D, which he and his wife had driven a total of 348,000 miles.

A former neighbor of mine, once a cab driver, had a 1967 Chevrolet sedan that was his taxi and his personal car for over 350,000 miles — and it was still going strong when he moved away.

It would be most interesting to hear from others who may know of cars that have surpassed these high-mileage records!

1954 GMC Peddler's Wagon

Both Chevrolet and GMC trucks (each manufactured by General Motors) included this canopy-style model in the 1954 line. It is typically associated, though, with a much earlier era of trucks, such as the 1921 Reo Speed Wagon.

GMC improved its six-cylinder OHV engine in 1954, and made minor improvements in the exterior and interior design.

Both Chevy and "Jimmy" (GMC) trucks had continued virtually unchanged from late 1947 until 1953 and were among the best built in bygone years. Many thousands were, and still are, in regular daily service.

The 1954 models were transitional — modified from the 1953 and earlier types, but unlike the newer models that appeared in the early months of 1955.

This so-called peddler's wagon was used to best advantage by itinerant produce peddlers who traveled through rural or suburban neighborhoods, where frequent stops were called for.

Many of these peddlers worked established fruit-and-vegetable routes, stopping at regular locations (or when hailed by customers). This unusual type of truck is still seen, but mostly in rural areas where there is no competition from supermarkets.

This kind of truck also symbolizes two things that should not be overlooked in these modern times: the small businessman and personalized service.

"Jimmy" was a nickname for any GMC truck, but in 1970 it became the name of a special small model, comparable to Chevrolet's Blazer.

1955 Chrysler "300"

"Va-rooom!" Here's a power-packed beauty of the mid-fifties, the era of the Great Horsepower Race. With 300 horsepower, the new Chrysler "300" series (introduced in January 1955) topped its rivals for a brief time. The initial models were all two-door hardtops.

All Chrysler Corporation cars were newly restyled for 1955 with "the Forward Look," and it was a most prosperous year for nearly all auto manufacturers, with all-new styling from most of them. Panoramic windshields, three-tone color schemes, and hot new V-8 engines were offered by many makes in 1955.

Only a thousand of the 1955 "300s" were planned, but the car was well received and more than seventeen hundred were built that year. For 1956, the new model had more horsepower and was known as the "300-B"; the letter suffixes continued each year until the "300-L" of 1965. (There was no "300-I," but in 1963 the letter skipped to J. The 1963 model was the scarcest; only four hundred were produced.) The most plentiful model was the "300-K" of 1964, with 3647 built.

The first "300" convertible was the "300-C" of 1957, and the hardtops were continued as before. In 1963, the "300" convertibles were skipped for a year.

Four-hundred-horsepower editions of this series were available in 1960 and 1961.

All of the Chrysler "300" types are in demand as collectors' cars.

1958 Chevrolet Impala

"Almost Too New to Be True?" The 1958 Chevrolet catalogue praised "the Most Exciting New Shape in a Generation of Cars?"

The trim, compact lines of the 1955–1957 Chevys were exchanged for a low, squat look, with bulgy curves and moldings that somehow recalled the style of the popular old 1936 Ford.

Whatever one thought of the 1958 Chevrolets, nearly all agreed that the "fat look" gave an air of solidity to the overall design.

The Impala, formerly a General Motors dream car, became the top-of-the-line Chevy two-door hardtop and convertible. From 1950 to 1957, the Bel Air had reigned supreme.

All the 1958 General Motors cars bore a strong family resemblance to one another, but Chevrolet alone sported the controversial new "gull-wing" rear fender sculpturing that made it instantly recognizable.

"Forward from Fifty" was a GM catchphrase in 1958, marking General Motors' Golden Anniversary.

Chevy's Turbo-Thrust V-8 engine featured wedge-shaped combustion chambers — within the block, instead of in the cylinder head.

New "Level-Air" suspension was optional, but air suspension was not successful at that time. The standard suspension was all-coil.

The Nomad was continued as Chevrolet's finest wagon; however, the 1958 model had four doors and lacked the long-windowed profile of the ever-popular 1955–1957 Nomads as well as the generous helping of brightwork.

Impalas had six lights at rear; lower-priced models had four.

The 1958 styling was offered for one year only. For 1959, all GM cars were completely restyled with the "linear" look: big windows and big tailfins.

1959 Cadillac

Motorists have mixed emotions about the 1959 Caddy. This was one of the most salient products of the late fifties because of its giant tailfins. Cadillac first introduced a modest fishtail effect on its rear fenders for 1948, and through the 1950s the fins grew — on Cadillac and on other brands that accepted the challenge.

The horsepower race and the rising of tailfins reached exciting new heights, and Cadillac's tallest fins were found on its standard assortment of 1959 models. But sharp rear fenders posed a danger to cyclists or skaters, who could collide with parked cars of this type.

With the new safety standards now in effect, we won't see any new cars with such appendages. Still, the 1959 Cadillac was a showy and ultra-glamorous "living-room-on-wheels," very big, and loaded with luxury features. If you like the looks of such a dreamboat, you may still be able to buy a clean one locally.

If you do, you'll be the envy of many. And strangers will come up to you and rave about your prize. But when you park it, for the sake of the neighbors' children, try to keep those unforgettable tailfins out of their path!

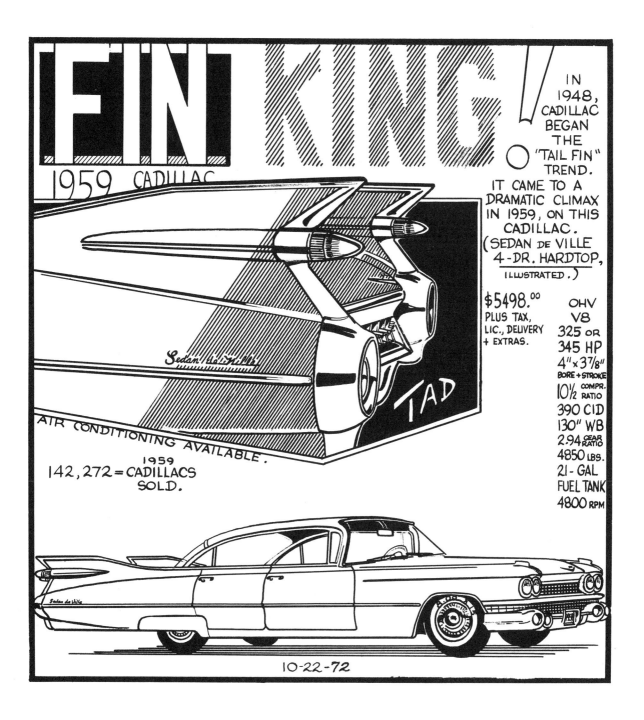

FIN KING!

1959 CADILLAC

IN 1948, CADILLAC BEGAN THE "TAIL FIN" TREND. IT CAME TO A DRAMATIC CLIMAX IN 1959, ON THIS CADILLAC. (SEDAN DE VILLE 4-DR. HARDTOP, ILLUSTRATED.)

$5498.00 PLUS TAX, LIC., DELIVERY + EXTRAS.

OHV V8
325 OR 345 HP
4" x 3⅞" BORE + STROKE
10½ COMPR. RATIO
390 CID
130" WB
2.94 GEAR RATIO
4850 LBS.
21-GAL FUEL TANK
4800 RPM

Sedan de Ville

TAD

AIR CONDITIONING AVAILABLE.

1959
142,272 = CADILLACS SOLD.

Sedan de Ville

10-22-72

The horsepower race of the fifties and sixties had finally led to various government safety controls and controls of engine emissions, and in 1972 the horsepower of most American cars was drastically reduced and many additional smog controls and the like were added. Nevertheless, 1973 was a prosperous year for American auto manufacturers, and the big V-8s enjoyed their last hurrah. Later that year, the world was hit with a sudden so-called energy crisis when the huge Arab oil cartels decided to grow richer and tighten the screws on the paying public. Thus 1973 was the last year for cheap and easily available fuel. Further complications arose as the energy crisis helped to create a new business recession and prices kept going up.

As a result of these problems, American cars were "downsized," and 80 or 85 became the top number on most speedometers (instead of 120 or 125). The big "dreamboat" cars of the late fifties and sixties soon looked like museum pieces, as they became outnumbered on the road by small, simple, fuel-efficient domestic and imported cars that usually were squarish and lacked any distinctive styling. One of the few truly unique designs was that of American Motors' Pacer.

The sixties began in comparative tranquillity. Democrat John F. Kennedy won the presidential election in 1960 and captured the imagination of the country with his Peace Corps and other social programs of the New Frontier. His assassination in November 1963 touched off a period of disillusionment, unrest, and rebellion.

In 1964, the Beatles, a British rock group, came to the United States, bringing on their heels many long-haired imitators. Some of the new rock and folk singers protested, in word and song, what they saw as social and political injustices. Much of the social unrest of the mid-sixties was aggravated by America's involvement in the Vietnam War, which escalated during the administration of President Lyndon B. Johnson. The issue of Vietnam hurt LBJ's popularity to the point where he finally chose not to run again in 1968. His Vice-President, Hubert H. Humphrey, was the 1968 Democratic candidate. But Republican Richard M. Nixon was elected.

The 1970s became an era of shortages and limitations. People all over the world had to pay more to get less. Even public services that were once free soon had a price tag. The Nixon administration suffered a stunning political humiliation when the Watergate scandal broke. As a result, Nixon stepped down in 1974 and handed control to his Vice-President, Gerald Ford. President Ford lost the election to Democrat Jimmy Carter in 1976. The 1980 election was won by Ronald Reagan.

Music fans were shocked in 1977 by the sudden deaths of two entertainment giants: Elvis Presley and Bing Crosby. Bing was older, but Elvis was barely past forty. By the 1960s, the old 78-rpm record was discontinued, and 45- and 33⅓-rpm discs had taken over (to be joined in the seventies by eight-track and cassette tapes). Among the songs of the 1960s and 1970s were "North to Alaska" (1960), "Moon River" (1961), "The Monster Mash" (1962), "Surfin' U.S.A." (1963), "I Want to Hold Your Hand" (1964), "What's New, Pussycat?" (1965), "Theme from *Dr. Zhivago* (Somewhere, My Love)" (1966), "Feelin' Groovy" (1967), "Love Is Blue" (1968), "Age of Aquarius" (1969), "Everything Is Beautiful (In Its Own Way)" (1970), "Where Do I Begin?" (1971), "The Candy Man" (1972), "Tie a Yellow Ribbon 'Round the Old Oak Tree" (1973), "Kung Fu Fighting" (1974), "Love Will Keep Us Together" (1975), "I Write the Songs" (1975–76), "You Light Up My Life" (1977), "It's a Heartache" (1978), "Disco Nights" (1979), and "Music Box Dancer" (1979–1980).

Limitations and a Growing Environmental Awareness

The 1960s and 1970s

1960 Rambler 6

This is the last model to be known, officially, only as the Rambler 6, for in 1961 this midline series became the Classic 6.

Don Wolfe, the owner of a 1960 model like this one, sent us a copy of his original sales invoice. The base price of the car (f.o.b. at factory) was $2383; the options were:

2-Tone Paint No. 2572	24.95
Automatic Transmission	199.50
Weather Eye Heater	76.00
Solex Glass	33.00
Reclining Back	25.50
Radio Inst. (Antenna Not Inst.)	75.65
White Tires	30.30
Undercoating	14.95
Back-Up Light	9.95
Antifreeze	4.00
Total Transportation Charged	65.50
Total Suggested Retail	$2942.30

The sales tax and annual license fee would also be additional. (The prices shown in these drawings are the minimum f.o.b., factory prices. Therefore, if you once bought a car similar to the one illustrated, you probably paid some 15 to 50 percent more because of added accessories, transportation to dealer, taxes, license, and so on.)

In a clever nationwide advertising campaign, Rambler's fuel economy was emphasized with a colorful series of full-page magazine ads: color photos of the cars plus cartoons by many of the nation's famous newspaper and magazine comic artists.

1961 Corvair Rampside Pickup

Chevrolet introduced its new rear-engine Corvair compact car late in 1959, for the 1960 season. A year later, three Corvair trucks were added to the line of cars. The new Model 95 trucks included a panel delivery van (the Corvan) and two pickups (the Loadside and this Rampside).

The Rampside displayed the advantage of side loading at the curb. The side door in the pickup bed unlatched and could be swung down to provide a handy ramp for wheeling or sliding heavy objects. It was an excellent idea, yet strangely enough, other truck manufacturers did not imitate it.

The Corvair trucks were discontinued in 1965, but the Corvair car was still in diminishing production until mid-May 1969.

What killed the rear-engined Corvair? Why was it shunned by most buyers after 1965? It was bad publicity, beginning with reports that the early Corvairs were unstable and liable to lose control easily. Nevertheless, true Corvair fans are fiercely loyal, and they have defended their favorite car against various written attacks.

General Motors improved the Corvair in the mid-1960s, but — as in the case of the 1958–1960 Edsel — unfavorable publicity drove off the buyers, despite vast improvements in each case.

Meanwhile, both Corvair and Edsel owners still drive and enjoy their cars, and most of them participate in the many activities of the clubs that have been formed for them.

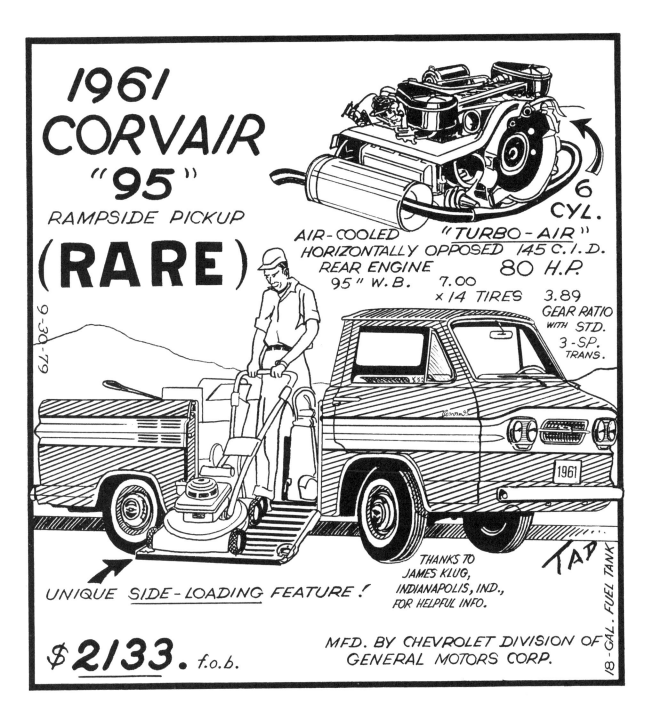

1961 Volkswagen

"It isn't so. That winding key you've been seeing on some VWs is not standard equipment. It's put there by proud Volkswagen owners, who go around telling their friends they get 40 miles on one winding. This isn't quite true. The correct figure is about 32 miles (regular driving), and it requires one gallon of gas. Otherwise, the winder gives you a pretty good idea of how economical it is to own and operate a Volkswagen." So read a Volkswagen ad of September 1960, when the 1961 model was making its bow.

These novelty keys, which attached to the engine compartment lid on the VW, got many a laugh in the 1960s. They stuck on the car by means of a rubber suction cup, and one mail-order house was selling them for as little as a dollar each! Because the so-called Beetle was a small, economical car, and because it had an old-fashioned, toylike profile, the key gave it an even "cuter" look than it already had.

The VW Type I, or familiar Beetle or Bug, as it was popularly called, was imported to the United States by the millions from the 1950s through the 1970s, and it was still available for a few years after the 1975 introduction of its more conventional replacement, the Rabbit.

Though the Beetle kept its same general body shape for many years, there were improvements and minor changes each year.

1963 Buick Riviera

In 1949, Buick introduced its first hardtop convertible, naming it the Riviera. But for 1963, an entirely new Riviera hardtop coupe was developed, with beautiful, angular, "knife-edged" (creased) styling. Sculptured ridges took the place of chrome strips. This Riviera heralded a new era in luxury sport models, or "personal" cars. Though the wheelbase was only 117 inches, its optional 425 c.i.d. V-8 engine packed a punch of 340 horsepower.

The Riviera of 1963 was luxurious throughout. Many were equipped with air conditioning, and "wood-grained" interior trim revived the atmosphere of the traditional classic car.

The 1963 Riviera was admired by all. Buick changed it but little during 1964. Disappearing headlights came along in 1965.

The 1963 Riviera sold for $4423 and up, f.o.b., factory; but the usual accessories, taxes, and so on brought the cost to well over $6000 in most cases. The 1963 model is mounting in resale value as a collector's car. And though some of the vehicles shown in these pages look strange today, the 1963 Riviera is still a beautiful car, even by current standards.

1963 BUICK "RIVIERA"

$4423.

325 OR 340 HP @ 4400 RPM

401 OR 425 CID V8

10.25 COMPRESSION

117" W.B. 4025 lbs.

3.42 OR 3.23 GEAR RATIO

63

TAD

11-8-81

BUICK

1963

1963 Chrysler Turbine Car

Fifty of these attractive cars were tested by two hundred individuals in 1963–1964 as the most dramatic of Chrysler's many gas turbine experiments.

The Turbine Car used a twin-regenerator gas-turbine engine and a modified TorqueFlite three-speed automatic transmission without torque converter.

The 130-horsepower turbine engine was comparable in performance to a 200-horsepower V-8, but it only weighed half as much and had one-fifth the moving parts.

It was smoother, quieter, and its exhaust was cooler and cleaner than that in conventional engines. It would start immediately in the coldest weather, with no warm-up period necessary. And no radiator was necessary.

There were no pistons or valve gear, and a single spark plug ignited the fuel.

The *fuel!* That was the real beauty of it, because the gas turbine engine would run on white gas, diesel oil, kerosene, aircraft turbine fuel, and the like. It sounds like just the kind of car we need today. Could this be the engine of the future?

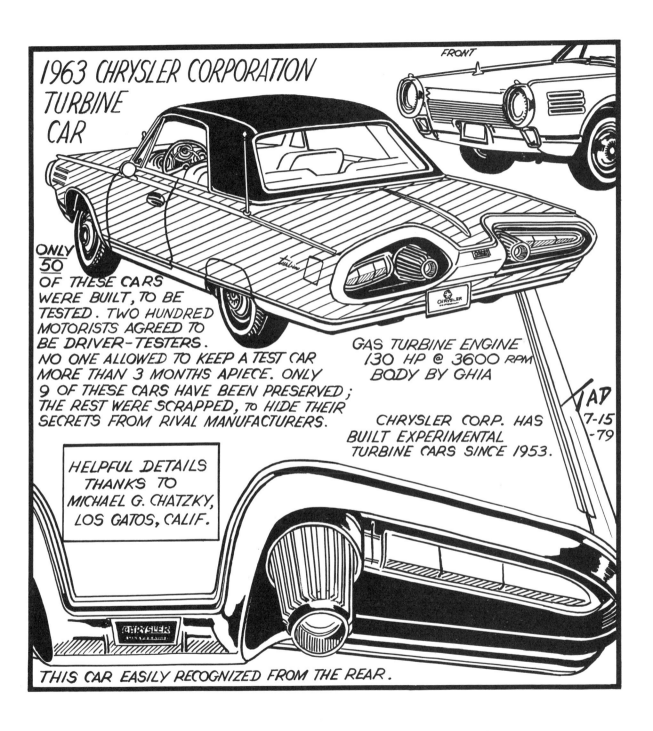

1963½ Ford

Question: "Were these later 1963 Fords really referred to as 1963½ models by the manufacturer?"

Answer: "Most definitely. And original catalogues, or ads from the leading magazines after February of 1963, will prove it."

In February 1963, the Ford Motor Company advertised its latest 1963½ models, with numerous improvements. The most notable styling change was on this newest hardtop, which closely resembled a convertible. Earlier, Ford had called such midyear surprises "spring models."

The 1963½ models were advertised in a splashy campaign, and in colorful magazine pages and spreads these Ford products were frequently shown in settings with a most attractive French Riviera background. Monaco and the Riviera had long been a world-famous tourist mecca, so why not present the latest Fords, Falcons, Fairlanes, and so on in a setting alluring to many?

As one ad in the *Saturday Evening Post* read: "Monaco is headquarters for the historic Monte Carlo Rallye — and for some of Europe's most sophisticated automotive types. Only great flair can turn heads in Monaco, but eyes followed this sleek shape wherever it went. A hardtop with the true convertible lilt . . ."

This car had bucket seats, a floor console, and a central console shift lever for both manual and automatic drive. A bench-seat version was also available.

Ford's enormous new 427 c.i.d. V-8 was a supermill, with "cross-bolting" to provide greater block and crankshaft rigidity as well as stronger connecting rods, a high-volume oiling system, a high-pressure fuel pump, valve spring dampers, aluminum intake manifolds, sonic-tuned headers, extruded aluminum pistons, and other performance goodies for this hot, large-bore (4.2346-inch) engine.

1964½ Barracuda

The styling of the all-new Barracuda was unique when it made its first appearance during 1964 (introduced in April, available for sale in May). In the front, it heralded the general styling of the following year's Valiant (the two cars shared the same chassis). At the rear, the Barracuda featured its sweeping "fastback," with a backlight more massive than that of any other contemporary car. The rear seats could be folded away to provide added luggage space or room for skis, surfboards, and such.

The new 273 c.i.d. V-8 was a good performer, which made speeds up to 108 miles an hour possible. There were also two "slant six" engines available (170 and 225 c.i.d., with 101 and 145 horsepower, respectively). The four-on-the-floor stick shift with Hurst linkage was optional with the V-8 or "225" six. The sport steering wheel was wood-grained, and the hubcaps (wheel covers) could be either "magnesium-type" with exposed chrome-plated wheel lugs, or in a ribbed style, with simulated "knock-off" hubs.

That huge rear window was, of necessity, tinted; and tinted glass was optional elsewhere.

Chrysler Corporation cars in 1964 offered an attractive 5-year-or-50,000-mile warranty on parts and workmanship. Some time ago I took a survey to determine how many people had driven their cars 200,000 miles or more. A large percentage of those who responded were owners of the Chrysler-built cars of 1962 to 1966. Of course, the early Barracudas have always been scarce and are of interest to collectors.

DASH

A NEW SPORT HARDTOP
INTRO. SPRING, 1964
BY PLY./VALIANT
DIV. OF
CHRYSLER
CORP.

1964½
BARRACUDA

273 C.I.D. V8
O.H.V. engine (3.63" × 3.31 BORE and STROKE)
180 HP @ 4200 RPM
8.8 COMPRESSION

(6-CYL. MODELS ALSO)

106 " W.B.

STD. 6.50 × 13
TIRES
WT.= 2905 lbs.

18-GAL. FUEL TANK

$2801.

TAD
6-26-77

4-ON-THE FLOOR
MANUAL TRANSMISSION with
HURST COMPETITION LINKAGE
OR AUTOMATIC 3-SP. Torque Flite
TRANS. WERE AVAIL. OPTIONS.

FEATURING
THE MOST
GIGANTIC *
"BACKLIGHT"
(REAR WINDOW) OF
ANY MODERN
"FASTBACK"!
(*-14.4 SQ. FT.)

1967 Corvette

Here it is, a very popular milestone in a long line of popular Corvettes. The 1967 model was the final example of the 1963–1967 styling cycle for Corvette, and the most refined. New for 1967 was the triple-2-barrel 435-horsepower version of the 427 c.i.d. engine, with a new hood for Corvettes with the big V-8s.

The parking brake was moved to the console; the interior was new; and at the rear there was a new wide back-up light.

A practical safety feature was the set of four-way hazard warning flashers, introduced on many other cars in the following years.

The two basic 1967 models were the Sting Ray fastback (first introduced in 1963) and this convertible. The convertible was equipped with a detachable hard top or with a folding canvas top. Some buyers chose to have both tops and alternate them as the spirit moved them.

Manfred A. Braun, who helped gather information on the '67 Corvette, writes that the un-advertised aluminum L-88 engine option was new and that cars so equipped came without radios or heaters and were intended mainly for off-road racing. "Only a handful of these cars were built," writes Braun, "and they are pure gold to collectors."

In the mid-1950s, Chevy's Corvette and Ford's Thunderbird were both sports cars. Within a short time, however, the T-bird shed its sports car image and became a luxury car. But the Corvette remained a true sports car, and has continued to use a fiberglass body (as it did when it was introduced back in 1953).

1967 Cougar

The scenic Monterey Peninsula of California, with cypress trees leaning toward the sea, is an ideal background for this car, because some of the very first 1967 Mercury Cougars were sold in Monterey.

The new Cougar for 1967 was Lincoln-Mercury's version of Ford's immensely popular Mustang, though the Cougar was longer and more luxurious. Animal names were "in" for pony cars of the sixties. The Jaguar, for example, was a popular British car desired by both the sporting crowd and the sophisticate. Another cat name seemed a good choice for a newcomer. And Ford had already manufactured a dream car called the Cougar II three years earlier. Contrary to the usual procedure, Cougar I followed Cougar II!

Remember those TV commercials with the live cougar sitting on top of a Lincoln-Mercury dealer's sign? The cougar, big cat that he was, would always give a defiant snarl at the right moment to emphasize the announcer's words.

Rumor had it that a trainer hidden behind the sign would pull the cougar's tail at the "appropriate" moment. The secret was not to pull the tail so hard as to bring on a confrontation!

The Cougar had a most artistic grille, with many parallel vertical pieces protruding crisply while neatly concealing the headlights. In perfect harmony, the taillights repeated this motif at the rear (with vertical ribbing) and were incorporated into attractive sequential turn signals in the style of the latest Thunderbird of that time. When the driver signaled for a turn, the light appeared to travel from the center to the right or left through the wide red band. It was like an animated neon sign, and auto buffs loved it.

The first Cougar was so beautiful that the 1967 styling was retained with little change in 1968. After all, too often a beautiful design was destined to be spoiled by overzealous stylists the following year.

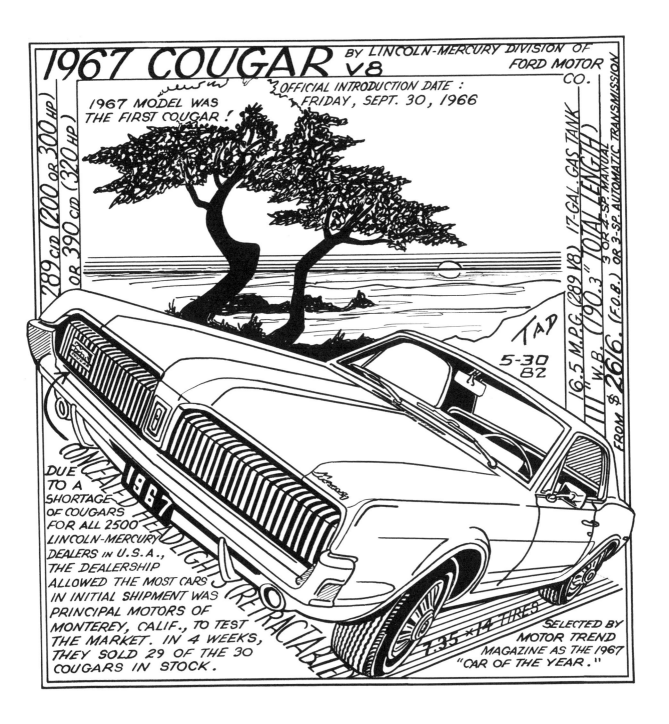

1968 Quasar-Unipower

This must be one of the strangest cars ever designed. With a body mostly of glass, it was shaped like a cube. Though this vehicle was built in England, the designer, a Vietnamese, was Quasar Khanh, and the car bore part of his name.

Looking like a rolling shower enclosure, the Quasar could seat up to five embarrassed people as it rolled past staring onlookers. Several people probably swore off drinking when they saw this thing go by!

Appearing as though it had been assembled from a collection of sliding glass patio doors, the Quasar had plenty of head room — but certainly no streamlining!

Designed for city use — and for anyone who didn't mind being laughed at — the boxy Quasar could still manage to attain a speed of about 50 if the wind was in the right direction. It was pushed along by a BMC transversely mounted rear engine and had automatic transmission.

One might expect that a flying rock could put a quick end to this freak-of-the-week, but the body was built of heavy safety glass and was reinforced at the corners by metal framing.

A heater was unnecessary, as a car with all this glass area would enjoy the benefits of natural solar heat. The roof panels were of tinted glass, in fact, to ward off an excess of sunlight.

1969 Dodge Charger

"Get Dodge fever! Buy a 1969 'White Hat Special'!" That was part of Dodge's ad campaign back in 1969, and the "White Hat Special" Dodge Charger included a vinyl roof in white (or black, tan, or green), simulated wood grain on the steering wheel, an outside remote control rearview mirror, white sidewall tires, "deep-dish" wheel covers, and more.

The Charger was introduced in 1966 as a powerful new two-door fastback, like the Barracuda and Marlin, but in two years it had adopted the "bustle back" typical of most other cars. Apparently the public liked the change, for in 1968 Charger sales climbed by an amazing 343 percent!

High-powered "muscle cars" were "in" back in 1969, and Dodge's hot ones were a part of the Dodge "Scat Pack," which had an aggressive-looking bumblebee mascot (an angry cartoon bee on wheels, wearing a crash helmet). Even the Dodge Coronet, usually a modest car for families, had a hot "Super Bee" model.

As for the White Hat advertising campaign, the "good guys" in Westerns traditionally wore white hats; thus, the boys down at your friendly neighborhood Dodge dealer's were "the boys in the white hats." (I don't recall many Dodge salesmen wearing such hats, however.)

Dodge also employed a pretty young female brunette model for many of their 1969 advertisements. This was the "Dodge fever" girl, and she often wore a white hat, too. All this may seem ridiculous today, just an interesting part of automotive history, but it seemed to be effective in an era when many people demanded more from their cars than just economical transportation.

TYPICAL NEW HOUSE OF 1969

new CONCEALED HEADLIGHTS

1969 DODGE CHARGER

225 CID 6 (145 HP) OR V8s OF 318, 383, 440 OR HEMI 426 CID V8 *

UNIQUE STEERING WHEEL

10-18-81

117" W.B.

7.35/7.75 × 14 TIRES (OR F70 × 14) 3142 TO 3710 lbs. R/T, R/T S.E. OR "500" MODELS ALSO AVAIL.

REAR DETAILS

* UP TO 425 H.P. @ 5000 RPM

FROM $3371.

TAD

1969 Lectra-Haul M-200

Just look at this truck! It is three stories tall and uses a diesel locomotive engine!

The Lectra-Haul off-highway dump truck was built in Tulsa, Oklahoma. The first trucks were shipped to Kaiser Steel Company's open-pit mine near Michel, British Columbia, and put into five-day-a-week, 6000-hour-a-year service. They were built to last fifteen years and were expected to operate from 15,000 to 20,000 hours before a major overhaul would be necessary. In fact, up to 35,000 hours without an overhaul was believed possible.

Though designed as a 200-ton truck, the Lectra-Haul was capable of pulling a 250-ton load up a 9 percent grade at slightly more than 7 miles per hour. Motive power was diesel-electric. In addition to the turbocharged Electro-Motive Diesel (GM) engine, an Electro-Motive DC traction motor was a part of the power team. It plugged into the new W-200 wheel unit and drove at a 35.2:1 gear ratio through a double planetary gear system.

With its freakishly high deck and cab and its railings, steps, front-overhanging dump body, and so on, the Lectra-Haul somehow resembles a battleship. For sheer brute size and power, it has seldom been equaled; yet at idling speeds its diesel fuel appetite was only 2½ gallons an hour.

1969 Pontiac GTO Judge

"All Rise for the Judge!" Pontiac, seeking a new triumph in the "muscle car" race of the late sixties, released the GTO Judge in January 1969. A decal-decorated coupe in a flaming orange-red, it was a wild-looking machine with a 60-inch airfoil "spoiler" across the rear deck for stability at high speeds.

Its grille was black, and it had steel mag-type wheels. Power front disc brakes were optional, as was the hood-mounted tachometer and a rally gauge cluster.

Coupled to its big V-8 engine was a fully synchronized floor-mounted three-speed gearbox. Or you could get a mean close-ratio four-speed with Hurst shifter or even a three-speed Turbo Hydra-matic if you preferred.

Some conservative, older drivers may have called them "musclehead" cars, but the crop of high performers of the late sixties and early seventies were designed specifically for young people who had money and who wanted action. The muscle car was meant for those who had graduated from plastic model kits and slot cars and who were now ready for real wheels — and hot ones at that!

"Uncle" Tom McCahill reviewed the Judge in the April 1969 *Mechanix Illustrated* with his usual flow of colorful adjectives and comparisons. He believed it would have reached 140 miles an hour if not for its relatively low drag-racing gear ratio. And he found that the Judge had a quieter and more tasteful interior than the run-of-the-mill hot, but tinny, pony cars.

A slightly restyled Judge was offered again in 1970.

Old muscle cars are truly collectors' items. They're hard to find because production of such novelties was limited to begin with, and many specimens burned out at an early age after a short, hard life of drag racing.

1970½ Gremlin

American Motors' "subcompact" Gremlin was introduced on April 1, 1970. It was unique among all cars, American or imported, because of its peculiar shape: long in front, abruptly sawed off at the rear, with a hatch door. At first it looked like the front half of a larger car.

But the Gremlin was no "half car" in its performance. It came with a 128-horsepower, six-cylinder engine with overhead valves — considerably more engine than was offered in other cars of its class. Yet fuel economy was 25 miles per gallon under favorable conditions.

The base price was a pleasant surprise: only $1879 for the two-passenger model, without any "luxury" features. The Gremlin was designed to compete with the most popular import, Germany's Volkswagen, and this minimum price was just $40 above the VW's.

Despite its April Fool's Day introduction, the Gremlin was no joke. It offered the only completely new shape on the automotive scene in five years. This innovation in itself was an advantage.

With a tested top speed of 100, the Gremlin runs rings around most other minicars. And, as American Motors declared, "We started a small car revolution by coming out with America's first subcompact: the Gremlin. If you had to compete with GM, Ford, and Chrysler, what would you do?"

1970½ GREMLIN

INTRO. APRIL, 1970 BY
AMERICAN MOTORS CORP.
6-CYL. O.H.V. ENGINE
199 OR 232 CID,
128 OR 145 H.P.   96" W.B.

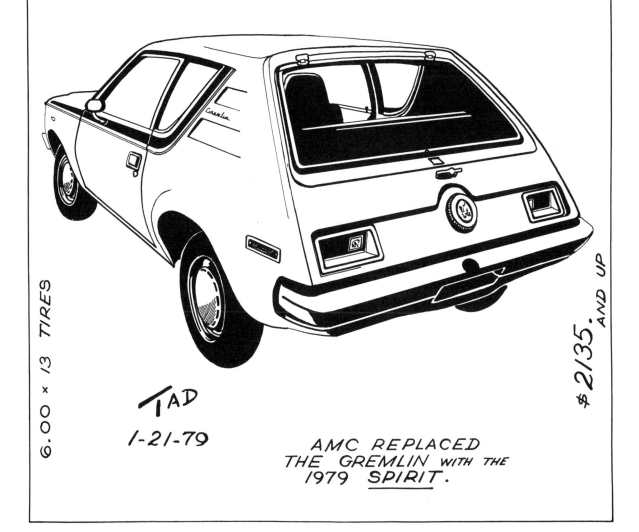

6.00 × 13 TIRES

$2135. AND UP

TAD
1-21-79

AMC REPLACED
THE GREMLIN WITH THE
1979 SPIRIT.

1975½ Pacer

I call this a 1975½ because it was not until the spring of 1975 that American Motors presented its dynamically styled wide compact car, the Pacer.

Richard A. Teague, the vice-president of styling for American Motors, was honored for his design work that led to the all-new car. Originally sketched as a hoodless, egg-shaped subcompact, the design evolved, before production, into something more acceptable to the public but still pleasing.

Not only was the Pacer strikingly new and unusually roomy, but its upholstery choices included novel Indian designs on the seat cushions!

In *Newsweek* (July 7, 1975) it was revealed that AMC had sold over 43,000 of the new Pacers during the first four months! The Pacer, in fact, accounted for 28 percent of AMC's total 1975 sales at that time, yet it hadn't even been available during the first few months of the season!

The car's only drawback was its mediocre gas mileage. With its aerodynamic styling, one expected an EPA average of 30 miles per gallon, but sometimes it was only 18 or less. A wagon was added to the Pacer line in 1977, but when the Pacers were restyled in front for 1978 they were less attractive. Because AMC likes to change its lines of cars periodically and introduce new names, the final Pacers were the 1980 models.